# Shakespeare Amazes in the Classroom

*Shakespeare Amazes in the Classroom* supports the instruction of learners needing to be challenged with content that is complex, rich, and of high interest to students, whether they are gifted, high achieving, or just curious about Shakespeare. Also a model of instructional design, *Shakespeare Amazes* is an exemplar of how comprehensive, standards-based instruction can be developed to meet the needs of gifted and talented learners.

Chapters consist of a collection of lessons that address specific learning goals related to point of view, character development, theme, comparing and contrasting, as well as multimedia interpretations, and other topics relevant to students studying fiction within grades four through eight. Chapters offer assessment suggestions, as well as strategies to support the social and emotional needs of students, the needs of multilingual learners, and tips for supporting twice exceptional students as they work through the lessons. The final chapter outlines, in detail, how the planning and implementation of a Shakespeare festival might be directed by students to maintain motivation, develop student agency, and allow for real world learning experiences to occur naturally alongside students' study of the Bard's words.

Online resources including editable critical thinking exercises, printable student texts, synopsis of the stories, comprehensive teaching notes, and example student–teacher conversations, as well as other bits of wisdom delivered with humor and supported by experience, are provided. Developed, taught, and revised over the past ten years using the *Understanding by Design* framework, this practical resource is sure to be a dog-eared teacher favorite for new and veteran educators.

**Jennifer Szwaya** has served several school districts in the suburbs of Chicago as a classroom teacher, a gifted specialist, and an instructional coach.

# Shakespeare Amazes in the Classroom

## Exploring the Bard with Gifted Students, Grades 4–8

Jennifer Szwaya

Routledge
Taylor & Francis Group
NEW YORK AND LONDON

Designed cover image: © Getty Images

First published 2024
by Routledge
605 Third Avenue, New York, NY 10158

and by Routledge
4 Park Square, Milton Park, Abingdon, Oxon, OX14 4RN

*Routledge is an imprint of the Taylor & Francis Group, an informa business*

© 2024 Jennifer Szwaya

The right of Jennifer Szwaya to be identified as author of this work has been asserted in accordance with sections 77 and 78 of the Copyright, Designs and Patents Act 1988.

All rights reserved. The purchase of this copyright material confers the right on the purchasing institution to photocopy or download pages which bear a copyright line at the bottom of the page. No other parts of this book may be reprinted or reproduced or utilised in any form or by any electronic, mechanical, or other means, now known or hereafter invented, including photocopying and recording, or in any information storage or retrieval system, without permission in writing from the publishers.

*Trademark notice*: Product or corporate names may be trademarks or registered trademarks, and are used only for identification and explanation without intent to infringe.

ISBN: 978-1-032-42079-0 (hbk)
ISBN: 978-1-032-36025-6 (pbk)
ISBN: 978-1-003-36110-7 (ebk)

DOI: 10.4324/9781003361107

Typeset in Palatino
by Deanta Global Publishing Services, Chennai, India

Access the Support Material: www.routledge.com/9781032360256

For Brian, Alan, and all of the humans like them.

May we find the time and energy to help them feel the power in their irreplaceable magic.

And, for all of the kiddos who experienced some version of the ideas in this book over the years:

St. Giles, Whittier, Tioga, and West Chicago friends, I hold you in my heart and cheer you on, always.

# Contents

*Foreword* . . . . . . . . . . . . . . . . . . . . . . . . . . . . . . . . . . . . . . . . . . . . . ix
*Preface* . . . . . . . . . . . . . . . . . . . . . . . . . . . . . . . . . . . . . . . . . . . . . . .xv
*Online Resources* . . . . . . . . . . . . . . . . . . . . . . . . . . . . . . . . . . . . xix
*Acknowledgments* . . . . . . . . . . . . . . . . . . . . . . . . . . . . . . . . . . . xxi

1 Getting Started – Overview and Planning . . . . . . . . . . . . . . . 1

2 Questioning, Annotating, and Answering
  to Comprehend. . . . . . . . . . . . . . . . . . . . . . . . . . . . . . . . . . . . 26

3 Elements of the Story – Plot, Character, Setting . . . . . . . . . 51

4 Theme. . . . . . . . . . . . . . . . . . . . . . . . . . . . . . . . . . . . . . . . . . . .87

5 Vocabulary and Word Choice . . . . . . . . . . . . . . . . . . . . . . .108

6 Point of View. . . . . . . . . . . . . . . . . . . . . . . . . . . . . . . . . . . . .141

7 Multimedia . . . . . . . . . . . . . . . . . . . . . . . . . . . . . . . . . . . . . .164

8 Comparing and Contrasting . . . . . . . . . . . . . . . . . . . . . . . .192

9 Shakespeare Festival . . . . . . . . . . . . . . . . . . . . . . . . . . . . . .212

*About the Author* . . . . . . . . . . . . . . . . . . . . . . . . . . . . . . . . . . . . . .231

# Foreword

## Tip of the 'Speare: A Student's Experience With and Advocacy for Shakespearean Education

*By Elijah Rivera, simultaneously introverted and outspoken high schooler and former student of Ms. Szwaya's*

The works of playwright William Shakespeare tend to be divisive in regards to their place in the school curriculum. Many will look back on their school years and remember the coverage of Shakespeare as a pompous drag of half-intelligible prose and vocabulary. They may look at Shakespeare's works as admittedly well-written but dated and unimportant, a pretentious holdover from many eras ago, and will shun his plays in favor of something seemingly more modern and "relevant."

Naturally, not everyone feels this way, not even among the children going through Shakespeare in class; some kids go on to take a great liking to Shakespeare's plays, taking up roles in their school plays for some of his most renowned works. They might even have a phase in their life where they attempt to insert Shakespearean cadence and language into their daily lives (a sort of phase they go on to regret). So, is it then fair to say that Shakespeare's works are completely worthless in the modern era of education? Of course not!

Putting aside whatever negative experiences you may have had with Shakespeare in the past, inserting Shakespeare into your courses can actually prove worthwhile, both for yourself and your students. Allowing young students to take steps in concepts like iambic pentameter and Aristotelian appeal, the reality of Shakespeare's scripts is that they were never truly meant for a student to take, sit down, read, annotate, and analyze alone;

that's a quick way to leave a sour taste in students' mouths. Above all, Shakespeare's plays are to be indulged in, to be watched or acted! This approach makes your English class better for everyone involved. Picking up this book means there's a decent chance you've at least considered the idea, so you're willing to be swayed and therefore you can be. Explaining the finer "how and why" of covering Shakespeare in class is what the rest of this book is for, but allow me to give the concept of "why" a kickstart.

A brief survey was conducted by the author about some of her students' experiences with Shakespeare. The survey wasn't exactly "scientific" *per se*, but all of the respondents had participated *actively* in Shakespeare in some form with the author. They had this to say on the memories they made working with Shakespeare.

> **What was your best memory of studying Shakespeare in Ms. Szwaya's class?**
>
> I found that coming together as a group to decode Shakespearean language really challenged me to put my critical thinking skills to use. It was like putting together puzzle pieces, once you fill in most of the puzzle, the rest comes along pretty easily.
>
> Steven W.
>
> Putting on a production instead of just reading Shakespeare heightened my learning experience a lot and made reading a complicated text a lot simpler.
>
> Leona J.
>
> I really enjoyed being creative with making the props for the play we did on *A Midsummer Night's Dream*. It was a fun experience.
>
> Amal A.

The right story and experience can really have a profound impact on peoples' lives. Here are some responses on how Shakespeare affected them, both academically and personally.

**How do you think exploring Shakespeare helped you as a student and as a person?**

Learning Shakespeare not only helped my young self to learn about important themes and life lessons, but it also helped me develop my own personality. Being able to take creative liberties in writing abridged versions of original Shakespeare was a key part of developing a creative mind.

*Diannah J.*

As a current sophomore, we've begun exploring Shakespeare even more. Being able to explore it earlier in your gifted class was really nice as I already am somewhat familiar with his language. Exploring Shakespeare also helped me with the morals taught in his stories. He taught me to think about my actions and not rush into decisions too quick like Romeo and Juliet.

*Adam T.*

**How did exploring Shakespeare make you feel?**

I found it very enjoyable. I especially was hooked on the fact that Shakespeare's works always had a meaningful message behind the confusing language that Shakespeare used. However, the most memorable moment consisted of teaming up with my friends to figure out what Shakespeare's theme was; what his message was to the reader (or viewer considering most of his works were presented as a play).

*Steven W.*

It made me really excited, though I did have some bias with previously liking Shakespeare, exploring sides of literature that I hadn't been introduced before and embracing the texts in new ways made me excited to learn about it.

*Leona J.*

Some are even willing to advocate for the future generations' exposure to Shakespeare!

**Why do you think it is important or helpful or enjoyable for kids to explore Shakespeare before high school?**

His stories are just downright interesting. They're also somewhat gruesome or darker, which in my personal experience is more interesting than a "regular" story. Fight scenes are interesting and if a teacher makes fun activities revolving around his stories it can be a lasting memory, like the play that we had in our own gifted class.

*Adam T.*

Analyzing and trying to understand Shakespeare can be difficult, even for advanced thinkers, so having the opportunity to try it out as a young kid is pretty amazing as a head start. The rewarding feeling after it finally clicking is truly worth it!

*Amal A.*

It could teach them life lessons from the stories they read, and they could expand their vocabulary with Shakespeare's word choice.

*Tony W.*

**What other insights would you like to share with teachers who may be considering exploring Shakespeare with their students?**

There is a reason why we learn so much Shakespeare in high school. His works are the textbook definition of a perfect story. It is important for young minds to capture the feel of a Shakespeare story arc so they can be inspired to write for themselves!

*Diannah J.*

I'd say do it. In my accelerated English class right now we just finished reading *Julius Caesar* and it was honestly very interesting. As long as teachers don't make it boring by just forcing us to read, Shakespeare's stories can be really enjoyable. Doing activities that aren't monotonous or just writing essays is also a really nice way to make students enjoy a story more. A student will love a teacher and remember them for a long time if they actually make class FUN and not just work.

*Adam T.*

It can be overwhelming at first, seeing the confusing and old language, so help kids out as they are becoming familiar with it and let them know it's not supposed to be easy.

*Amal A.*

I would definitely start as early as possible. Although the language may seem intimidating at first, (especially for a grade school student) creating those skills to decode and understand are essential to a child's development academically. Most of schooling is figuring things out and emphasizing that independence and group teamwork would definitely be beneficial to a child's development.

*Steven W.*

Something to keep in mind is that these students are in high school. The stereotyping of kids and teenagers as absentminded candy quaffers and apathetic, tech-addicted autopilots, respectively, is partially a result of their role models refusing to adapt to their minds (and partially due to hormones). Here we can see though, a bunch of high schoolers singing high praises for Shakespeare, and all of that is well due to the fact that their class handled the teachings of Shakespeare so well. I too belong to this group, and without being too overbearing, what I can say is that the chance to delve into Shakespeare in such a way at a young age allowed me to break my boundaries in terms of consuming literature, as well as learn about many fascinating concepts early on. It's clear then that Shakespeare doesn't need to be a miserable experience, and that his plays can be fun and unforgettable (in the good way) for participants! But as a quality photograph requires the right angle, so too does a quality English class. This book is written for the curious, such as yourself, to help catch that and shed the perceived antiquity of Shakespeare so that his timelessness can shine through.

# Preface

After lots of agonizing I decided to start this book the same way that I end most classes: By asking a question. Inquiring with an eye roll in what has become a class favorite: The dramatization of a bored kid as performed by a chubby, frighteningly enthusiastic lady over 40, I huff out loud, "Who even cares?!?! Who eeeeeeven cares about thiiiiisssssuuuuh." This routine has become shorthand for a regularly occurring conversation. It happens in whole group discussion, or informally as students transition between subjects, or during partner reflections. We discuss what they learned, and why their learning matters, so they understand why they should, or could, care. I have found this routine to be essential to creating a level of engagement that drives students towards agency in their learning. And, as I have been working on this book it is the question asked most frequently by curious friends: Why Shakespeare for intermediate and middle school students? What's the point? So, let us start there. Exploring Shakespeare with mid- to upper-grade school children. Why bother? Who even cares?

Shakespeare's work is a cornerstone of our culture. When I say "our" I am referring to all humans who speak English whether as a first, second, or 40th language. During the years I have worked to teach young people using Shakespeare's texts I have encountered countless references to the Bard in the world beyond our classroom. In the past three months alone I have come across several. A friend texted a screenshot of a page from one of Rachel Renée Russell's *Dork Diaries* series in which *A Midsummer Night's Dream* is a part of the plot. In physician and author Gabor Maté's book about addiction titled *In the Realm of Hungry Ghosts,* when describing his patients as struggling to release themselves from the destructive grip of addiction he compares them to *Julius Caesar*'s "Young Cassius" who "has a lean and hungry look." Netflix released a film titled *Rosaline* told from the perspective of Romeo's heartthrob with whom he was obsessed immediately before Juliet. An advertisement for a local theater company performing *Hamlet* set in Harlem, New York passed through my Facebook feed. These examples illustrate the fact that Shakespeare is everywhere – as a funny allusion, an illustration to a point made in another field entirely, and a continuing source of cultural creation even still. Without awareness and exposure, such cultural connection might go unnoticed or unappreciated, which is not the worst thing in the world, but it certainly deprives one of access to participating in and being enriched by the many avenues on which Shakespeare appears in our culture. For this reason, using Shakespeare in the classroom to reach grade level learning goals can be considered an act of social justice as it gives students access to and ownership of the greatest writer in the English language, who also happens to be a consistent cultural reference in the English speaking today.

One might argue that the literature canon is already overstocked with old white men, and I would agree. However, it is hard to argue that any other old white guy's writing deserves a space in our common cultural canon more than Shakespeare. The culture of the world's English-speaking population and beyond must agree, as according to Wikipedia's listings, *A Midsummer Night's Dream*, *Romeo and Juliet*, and *Hamlet* alone have been restaged, reinvented, and reimagined hundreds of times. Of these productions many are adaptations from countries such as Japan, India, and Mexico. The universal tales Shakespeare tells grip the human heart across miles and centuries. Our students deserve access to the party.

What party? I'm speaking of the joy that comes from making meaning of rich language, examining conflicts that resonate, uncovering deep personal significance that helps students connect with other creators over time. Students, and especially gifted learners, enjoy complexity and solving puzzles. In addition to the puzzling language, the types of conflicts in Shakespeare's stories demonstrate respect for our learners that resonate with them leading to a more engaged classroom. Students know the conflicts in Shakespeare are true to life – tragic things happen and we have to wrestle with our worst selves as Hamlet does. People make bad decisions that lead to unimagined consequences as in *Romeo and Juliet*. And, as in *A Midsummer Night's Dream*, people act out of jealousy and anger – even good friends. These themes resonate with our students because they resemble what the kids know to be true about life. I believe that the complexity in language and the honesty about life's difficulties make students more responsive to working with Shakespeare because the texts honor their intelligence and are respectful of the fact that students see and know more about life than we give them credit for. When compared to discussions prompted by less complex text, teaching Shakespeare was a more celebratory experience because the challenge respected their intelligence, and thus they saw it worthy of their effort.

Consider a conversation I had in a coffee shop with a curious friend who asked, "Aren't teachers too scared to teach Shakespeare?" I think that fear in particular can set us free. Scholars today debate over the shades of meaning within Shakespeare's texts. The fear of not being right is less acute when one realizes just how many people over how many centuries have participated in deciphering and interpreting Shakespeare's words. Rather than fearing being wrong, one can opt to join the puzzle solving bonanza that is reading Shakespeare. The key is to support one's thinking using the text as evidence. And this skill – supporting a claim with text evidence – is the crux of what students in contemporary reading classrooms should be doing to increase comprehension. Shakespeare gives kids a rigorous mess to make meaning of. Because it is a mess that the teacher feels less comfortable solving for their students, those students get to operate on a level closer to the teacher since they are both in the mess together. Students sense this and it yields a type of alchemy turning reading classes that were previously based on an entrenched power dynamic – teacher as distributor of knowledge. And because, as one fourth grader of mine said, "Shakespeare is so grownuppy."

I find it helpful to routinely ask myself the "who cares?" question as a teacher as well. Who really cares if there is one more book on Shakespeare? One more instructional manual for teachers? What makes this endeavor worthwhile? In reflecting on this, three answers powerfully respond. One, the unit in this book was developed using the *Understanding by Design* framework

(Wiggins & McTighe, 2008) and integrates multiple standards, so it serves as a model for writing such a unit. Lesson planning is a complex task, and is getting more complex. As an instructional coach the question I get most often is "how?" This unit is one tiny answer to that question in that it provides an exemplar. Two, this project has been cultivated over years of practice, flop, and revision. It's been a funny and powerful learning journey that might inspire you to persist in finding your passion for teaching if, like me, you had misplaced it. Three, the most compelling reason why exploring Shakespeare with elementary students is worthwhile is because in every iteration I have seen magic happen with this unit. Engagement, teamwork, innovation, creativity, and enthusiastic mastery sparkle and crackle in the classroom every time the Bard has joined us. I hope similar alchemy occurs for you and your students.

# Online Resources

Keep an eye out for the online resources mentioned throughout this book (in the order below). These resources can be downloaded, printed, used to copy/paste text, and/or manipulated to suit your individualized use. You can access the downloads by visiting this book's product page on our website: www.routledge.com/9781032360256 (then follow the links indicating related resources, which you can then download directly to your computer).

- Annotation worksheets for:
  - William Shakespeare's *A Midsummer Night's Dream*, adapted from Mary and Charles Lamb's 1807 retelling.
  - William Shakespeare's *Romeo and Juliet*, adapted from Mary and Charles Lamb's 1807 retelling.
  - William Shakespeare's *Hamlet, Prince of Denmark*, adapted from Mary and Charles Lamb's 1807 retelling.
- Selections from:
  - *A Midsummer Night's Dream* by William Shakespeare.
  - *Romeo and Juliet* by William Shakespeare.
  - *Hamlet, Prince of Denmark* by William Shakespeare.
- Critical Thinking: Questioning and Answering document.
- Three-panel comic strip.
- Critical Thinking: Scamper Chart.
- Critical Thinking: Checking In With Characters.
- Critical Thinking: Shakespeare's Botanicals.
- Critical Thinking: Translating the Bard.
- Critical Thinking: Perspective Graphic Organizer.

# Acknowledgments

Many thank yous and smothering hugs are owed to the following people.

Nicole, Kristy, Marie, Dara, Jess, and Alexandra: Thanks for wading through the first drafts to provide invaluable feedback. That was a tedious task. Thanks for seeing it through.

Rebecca at Taylor Francis Group: What an amazing support you have been. Thank you for the feedback that kept me motivated and reflecting critically, and for supporting this quirky voice I have to offer.

Lisa: You are the best cheerleader a sister could ever ask for. Thank you for filling my bucket over and over.

Holly and Karen: Thank you for the co-working sessions. Your companionship got me through some uncomfortable mental spaces this year.

Katelynn McAllister: Thank you for the graphic design work. Your expertise, speed, and professionalism would be a benefit to any project.

Thanks to all colleagues at St. Giles, Whittier, Tioga, and West Chicago. Learning from you and growing with you has been a most rewarding journey.

To all of the leaders that gave me the space and trust to try some wacky things over the years: Sue, Carol, Nicole, Carlos, and Mark. Thank you for supporting and encouraging my growth as an educator.

Darren, for making it all possible. You are my light. I am most definitely the lucky one.

# 1

# Getting Started

## Overview and Planning

Shakespeare has taught me that interest inventories are a powerful tool. I administer the surveys a few times a year to gather information about student likes, dislikes, and curiosities. The information helps me make instruction more responsive and engaging. One particular year, my fourth grade class discovered the Shakespeare Insult Generator, an online treasure that generates Shakespearean style insults such as, "Thou mewling swag-bellied flap dragon," and were in love with it. I had many survey respondents reply "Shakespeare!" when asked what topics they might be interested in reading about in that class. Those survey results collided with the boredom I was feeling teaching the same reading content for the fourth consecutive year, so I got to planning.

The first year I only introduced fluency activities, but we had so much fun that I decided to expand when I took a new position teaching gifted and talented learners in grades K–5. This position allowed me to create a curriculum from scratch. The year that I developed and taught the first version of this project, students were again as enthused as my previous class had been. When these students were introduced to the fact that they would be exploring the Bard, I received a chorus of *ooooohs*, wide eyes, and actual squeals. One student swooned, "Shakespeare is so grownuppy!" After ten years, I have yet to have a year where

DOI: 10.4324/9781003361107-1

at least three-quarters of the class isn't immediately impressed and excited at the thought of learning about Shakespeare and his writing. And, when I explain that they will soon begin planning for a Shakespeare Festival as well, and describing all that entails (performing, set design, technology, fight scene choreography, costumes, music, publicity, advertising, etc.) the other quarter of students have been won over. The reason for the consistently positive response from students is due, in part, to the level of enthusiasm I bring to the lessons, but more importantly, I've come to learn that it is a matter of being seen. Often our bright, odd-bird students, who crave to create and philosophize, do not feel seen by teachers. Exploring Shakespeare says "I see you and your complexity." Feeling seen allows space for other emotions like enthusiasm and excitement to come out and play. Your enthusiasm for the content and the energy with which you present that content makes it all possible.

> Exploring Shakespeare says, "I see you and your complexity." Feeling seen allows space for other emotions like enthusiasm and excitement to come out and play.

## Resource Overview

This resource was created to help you find amazing Shakespeare moments with your students. It is divided into nine chapters or modules. Chapter 1, this chapter, is an overview and includes tips for creating a Shakespeare exploration that works for your class. It also includes a summary of the anchor texts and ideas for anticipatory sets, which are initial lessons that get students engaged with content and familiar with important background knowledge prior to beginning the readings. Chapter 2 discusses how to engage students in asking and answering questions to comprehend. Chapters 3 and 4 provide strategies for investigating the elements of plot, character, setting, and theme. Chapter 5 delves into vocabulary while Chapter 6 jumps into ways to explore point of view. Chapter 7 explores Shakespeare through the media of music, film, and art. Chapter 8 provides an overview of comparing and contrasting, and Chapter 9 discusses in detail how to produce a Shakespeare Festival with students that includes a performance and a museum of student learning. Chapters 1 and 9 are important to read carefully before you start to plan your own unit of study. I suggest reading Chapter 1, this chapter, then skimming through Chapters 2–8 to get the gist of the learning activities before finally slowing down again to read Chapter 9. This process will help clarify how this text works as a teaching resource, and how it might best be used to meet the needs of your learners in the time you have available.

This chapter is the guide to getting ready to explore Shakespeare with your students. It includes an explanation of the structure of the chapters, resources included with this text, the research rationale behind the learning activities, tips for using the text, summaries of the Shakespearean texts included in this resource, as well as ideas and lessons for getting started with a unit of study that explores the Bard. Chapter 9 is all about the Shakespeare Festival, which in my experience is the engine that drives students to persevere through the more challenging aspects of reading Shakespeare's language. The chapter features important information about student projects, planning a festival given the time available to you, how festival planning meetings can be organized, and key planning considerations.

For ease of use, the chapters each include the following components.

## Narrative

The narrative section offers anecdotal support for the learning goals related to the chapter. The information shared either illuminates a tangential instructional technique, which may not be directly related to Shakespeare, but that is helpful in reaching the instructional goals for the chapter and across this resource.

## Learning Goals

The learning goals section of each chapter describes the learning outcomes for the activities in the chapter. Goals are based on the Common Core Standards, but are applicable to learning environments that do not rely on the Common Core Standards for learning progressions. Goals are described in this section and "I can" statement examples are provided to assist teachers in communicating learning goals to students. Learning goals are also described by a simple chart in each of the chapters. While the rubric is not robust enough to be used to assess final products, it is intended to aid students in goal setting. In reviewing the provided rubrics, students have options to go far or go deep. The "go far goal" can be set by looking across the rubric which arranges learning goals from the fourth-grade level to the eighth-grade level. Students can read the goals across to determine where they are currently working, and what level they would like to strive towards. Students can also read down to select activities which ask them to deepen their understanding of the learning goal via extension activities related to the learning goal.

## Assessments

Each chapter features assessment suggestions. In order to seamlessly meet the expectation that students be prepared for standardized assessments, it has been my preference to assess progress towards learning goals by using text dependent questions (TDQs) that also support students in preparing for written responses on district-wide and standardized assessments. Text dependent questions are those that require students to make a claim, support it using evidence from the text or texts, and explain how their claim is supported by the selected evidence using reasoning. For this reason, the assessment section provides information on how to assess using text dependent questions. Though Module 1 discusses text dependent questions and the question–answer relationship, *Shakespeare Amazes* assumes that students have experience making claims and supporting them with text evidence. If this skill is not within your student's skill sets, then I advise tightening that up first. However, note that any of the activities can be used as assessments as well. In my experience, rubrics work best when they are designed in collaboration with students, so for this reason, there are no rubrics in this resource.

In a perfect world, assessment of student learning would occur in two mini conferences. At the start of a module, students meet with the teacher to review the learning goals and identify the goal that they would like to achieve. They then discuss with the teacher the learning activities for the module, and begin to consider what activities they might do to go deeper with their learning. Students also review the text dependent questions for the module so that they know about the target they need to hit before instruction even begins. Over the course of instruction for the module, students gather evidence to share at the conclusion of the module to prove that they achieved the specified learning target. During a concluding conference, students share their evidence and work to persuade the teacher that they have reached the desired target.

## Activities
Each chapter features several learning activities that support the learning goal described for that chapter. The activities are written with optimum conditions in terms of time. We know that time is not always available in the quantities we'd like, so feel free to adjust the activities as necessary to accommodate the constraints of your classroom and teaching circumstances. I have definitely done so over the years.

## Considerations
Classrooms are complex spaces filled with unique learners. For this reason, strategies or lesson adaptations incorporated to meet the needs of diverse learners have been included when there is wisdom to share from my own experience. However, considerations described in chapters are by no means a comprehensive resource, so be sure to incorporate your own wisdom and knowledge of the students in your class as well.

## Essential Question
This instructional unit has been designed using the backwards design process developed by Grant Wiggins and Jay McTighe, thus the essential question is a key component of this unit's design. The essential question is: What is the power of language? This question was selected for several reasons, the primary being to address students' lethargy with reading and writing that seems to appear around fifth grade. At this point in school students are reading and writing to learn, rather than learning how to accomplish the mechanical process of reading and writing. I have found that it is in this intermediate part of school life that students need to discuss the purpose, or power, in being skilled readers and writers in

order to remain motivated to continue striving in these areas. So, considering what power language brings to our lives at this point in their schooling is especially timely. Each learning activity also helps students discover ways in which language gives us power.

My strategy for revisiting the essential question throughout the unit is to dedicate a bulletin board or wall to an essential question mind map. At the start of the unit the essential question sits encircled on the board with spokes emanating from the center. Some spokes will be labeled with character names and others will be blank. During essential question discussions, the spokes labeled with characters' names will feature open spokes that are labeled with answers that character would give to the essential question. For instance, spokes not labeled with a character are reserved for insights and answers that come to students through their learning activities. New spokes and circles should be added with each discussion which could occur consistently across the study of Shakespeare.

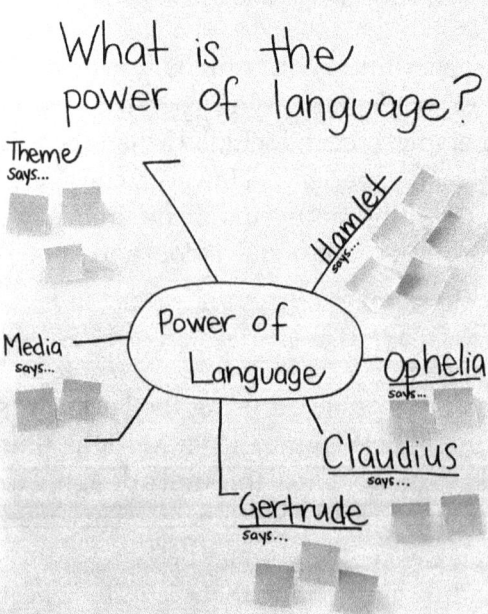

**FIGURE 1.1** A simple web can be constructed to capture student thoughts about how the texts relate to the essential question. These recorded thoughts can then serve as the research base for a final project in which students use the texts to answer the essential question.

## Anchor Texts and Resources

Although Shakespeare wrote dozens of texts, three were chosen to "anchor" student learning in this book: *Hamlet*, *Romeo and Juliet*, and *A Midsummer Night's Dream*. *Hamlet* was chosen because students, especially those in upper grades, can relate to Hamlet's relationships with the adults in his life. This is not to suggest that there are tons of kids running around whose uncle has murdered their father and married their mother! Rather, students can relate to Hamlet who uses his only power – the wit of his mind – to respond to the actions of his uncle and mother. Like Hamlet, kids in their 12th and 13th years of life especially tend to see the adult hypocrisies that were more easily hidden from them in their earlier years. Being powerless to actually effect some change they resort to sarcasm and snark to combat forces they are otherwise powerless over. Similarly, *Romeo and Juliet* is particularly engaging for adolescents because it deals with children who have defied their parents. It imagines what would happen if children were able to follow their impulses to adult conclusions. This is the fantasy of many students in typical preteen conflict with their families – what would happen if I just ran away and made all of my own decisions? Finally, *A Midsummer Night's Dream* was selected because it allows for magnificent settings to be created and, most importantly, it explores jealousy among friends and unfair parental demands, which are issues all kids can relate to.

This book features three categories of supplemental resources. In 1807, Mary Lamb and her sibling Charles wrote *Tales from Shakespeare* for children. The first supplemental resource for this book is based on their work. This first resource will be referred to throughout this book as the Lamb texts. This collection was intended to introduce children to the Bard's stories. The authors reconstructed the original dramas into a more familiar prose structure while using Shakespeare's vocabulary to the greatest degree possible. The choice to use this anthology was made for several reasons. First, it is an appropriate entry point to the works of Shakespeare while also being rigorous enough to challenge students. Second, exposure to Shakespeare through a narrative retelling allows students to become more comfortable with the plot, so that they have a schema in their minds when exploring Shakespeare's original text. Third, with Shakespeare's works being written in the late 1500s and early 1600s, the 1856 collection provides a stepping stone between modern language and Shakespeare's language which provides a wonderful opportunity to examine how language changes over time. The versions shared in this resource were edited for brevity, numbered for reference, and separated by tildes. The tilde designates where one act of the original Shakespearean play ends and another begins. This feature will help students align the text to Shakespeare's dramas which is useful as students seek text evidence in certain sections.

The second resource is based on Shakespeare's original works. This resource differs from Shakespeare's originals in that they have been drastically shortened without losing his most famous lines and while retaining enough text to allow students to investigate plot, setting, character, point of view, theme, and comparing and contrasting. This second resource makes reading and writing about Shakespeare more manageable, and throughout the text it will be referred to as the Shortened Shakespeare. A further benefit of the Shortened Shakespeare is that as students work to create their own production, they may use the Shortened Shakespeare document as a starting script that they then edit as needed. Students may opt to add more modern language or elements of their home languages, summarize some lines and have a narrator speak them, include more stage directions, or make other revisions based on what type of performance they are planning. Having an editable script to start with saves time and gets students to the interesting work faster. In addition, Chapter 7 focuses on multimedia. Film selections can be reviewed with the Shortened Shakespeare in hand so that students can make connections between the film and the Bard's original language. Lastly, should an additional resource be needed to support differentiation efforts, the entire text of all of Shakespeare's works can be found on multiple websites.

> Access the following digital resources at www.routledge.com/9781032360256:
> - Full text and annotation worksheets for:
>   - William Shakespeare's *A Midsummer Night's Dream*, adapted from Mary and Charles Lamb's 1807 retelling.
>   - William Shakespeare's *Romeo and Juliet*, adapted from Mary and Charles Lamb's 1807 retelling.
>   - William Shakespeare's *Hamlet, Prince of Denmark*, adapted from Mary and Charles Lamb's 1807 retelling.
> - Selections from:
>   - *A Midsummer Night's Dream* by William Shakespeare.
>   - *Romeo and Juliet* by William Shakespeare.
>   - *Hamlet, Prince of Denmark* by William Shakespeare.

## Research Rationale

The unit of instruction presented in this source was created using the principles of *Understanding By Design* (Wiggins & McTighe, 2008). The entire unit is designed around an essential question that is revisited repeatedly, and answered via the learning activities. The learning goals are discussed prior to the descriptor of the activities because good instruction is driven by the learning needs of students and designed with the end in mind. Thus, once the learning goals are identified, then the appropriate learning activities can be selected. Finally, students engage in a literal authentic performance to demonstrate the culmination of their learning.

The ideas for the activities in the following chapters came from three main sources. The first source from which activities were drawn is directly from the minds of amazing educators and education organizations. In these cases the source of the idea is cited within the activity. The second source is the genius of the collective teacher "mind hive" which allows wisdom gathered over years in education conversation, seminars, and graduate classes to spark ideas in the classroom. Of the ideas that are not attributed to a specific education genius's thought, I wish I could discern what exactly was inspired by the teacher "hive mind" and what ideas came directly from my own mind. Any lack of credit paid to the original mind was unintentional.

The activities selected and developed for this resource were chosen based on their alignment to specific, research-based practices. The research-based practices are as follows.

1. **Schema Theory**

    Schema theory describes how we organize information in our brain. According to Meta and Fine (2019), "Cognitive scientists think of deep learning – or what you might call 'learning for understanding' – as the ability to organize discrete pieces of knowledge into a larger schema of understanding." We create structures to help us organize incoming information to create a model of how things work, and those structures are indicative of deep learning. As we gain new knowledge, we connect that new knowledge to other things we know, learn, experience, and believe. Like a giant idea web in our mind, a schema forms in our brain. Because Shakespeare has such a presence in our language and culture, he makes a wonderful central hub to our schema. Shakespeare references are everywhere, so having Shakespeare as an integral part of their schema will allow it to remain active throughout life.

2. **Close Reading to Ask and Answer Text Dependent Questions**

    Another research-backed aspect of this resource is close reading and text dependent questions. Close reading and text dependent questions are the basis for developing comprehension, and used to promote rereading text in order to build schema (Fisher & Frey, 2012; Pearson & Johnson, 1978). Text dependent questions are also used to assess student acquisition of reading skills throughout this resource. Instructional research leader Doug Fisher describes close reading as the instructional practice of having students engage with a text over multiple readings so that they can critically examine the text, better understand it, and develop their personal schema (Fisher, 2012). Text dependent questions are questions that the reader might be asked, or ask themselves, about the text. TDQs are so connected to the text that evidence collected from the text is used to support the claim that answers them. Close readings paired with TDQs are especially effective in developing comprehension because how a student reads a text is influenced by the type of questions they are asked about it (Fisher & Frey, 2012; Fisher, 2012). For example, certain questions may not even require that the student reads the text. A thematic question related to *A Midsummer Night's Dream* might be, "What is required to create a trustworthy friendship?" While this question is certainly related to Shakespeare's work, it could be answered without having to read the text. Text dependent questions are different in that they require the student to return to the text for answers. So, a TDQ version of the previous question might be reframed as, "How would you describe the level of trustworthiness present in Hermia and Helena's friendship?" Such questions lead to more significant engagement with the text, and thus improved comprehension. Teachers are often the question writers in the classroom, however, in close readings where students are the question generators, students are also developing their ability to think critically (Fisher & Frey, 2012). Close reading's structure gives the time and attention needed to let students practice these highly transferable skills that can help them better understand not only Shakespeare's work, but any text.

3. **Productive Struggle**

    Productive struggle is the idea that students must experience a Goldilocks level of challenge when learning in order to grow. That is, the challenge should be significant enough to be felt, but not so intense that it is discouraging (Kerr & Booth, 1978; Tomlinson, 2005). The activities throughout this resource provide opportunity for productive struggle, and greater academic growth. Productive struggle is important because without struggle students get bored. Boredom, according to Fisher, Frey and Hattie (2016), can result in negative growth for a student.

4. **Peer Collaboration and Discussion**

    Student learning increases when collaboration, team work, and discussion are aspects of their learning – especially when "a jigsaw approach" is used. According to research done by

Fisher, Hattie, and Frey on the effect sizes of various instructional strategies, classroom discussion has an effect size of 0.82; cooperative learning has an effect size of 0.59 (2016). According to their research, any effect size over 0.4 is significant in terms of the potential for accelerated student growth. Jigsaws have an effect size of 1.2, which means if used regularly students have the potential to make three years' worth of academic growth in the span of one year. Throughout this resource, the jigsaw method is adapted to allow students to deeply engage with an aspect of the text in collaboration with peers before discussing as a class, and then sharing out findings with the greater group.

5. **Student Agency**

    Students must be active participants in their own education. This may come in the form of choice being embedded in instructional design, student goal setting, portfolio assessments, and the role of student as creator in the Shakespeare festival. Research has shown that students who are engaged in the process of learning are more successful academically (Buchmann & Steinhoff, 2017; Wigfield, Eccles, Fredricks, Simpkins, Roeser, & Schiefele, 2015; Otis, Grouzet, & Pelletier, 2005; Wang & Eccles, 2011), they experience learning that is more personally and socially rewarding (Shawer, 2010); and they are more likely to choose challenging learning experiences that they do not give up on (Johnston, 2004).

6. **Teacher Clarity**

    According to Fisher, Hattie, and Frey (2016) teacher clarity and credibility have an enormous impact on student outcomes. When speaking of teacher clarity and credibility we are referring to a teacher's ability to engender a sense of trust, competence, and ability to deliver instruction dynamically. Teachers who are clear and credible know their content and feel confident and enthused about students mastering that content, and students know it. In order to support teacher clarity and credibility several tools have been added to this resource to support teachers in their efforts to master the stories covered in this text. First, the story summaries in Chapter 1 provide a brief overview. Second, the Lamb narrative stories can familiarize teachers with the plot of the stories. The edited Shakespearean versions provide a focused and scaled down version of Shakespeare's original language. Finally, the *No Fear Shakespeare* series is an external resource that can help teachers become more secure in discussing Shakespeare's language as it provides modern language translations of Shakespeare's words.

## Tips for Using This Book

Throughout my career teaching in gifted programs, I have encountered extremes in the amount of instructional time. In one district I worked to enrich fourth and fifth graders once or twice a week for class periods that lasted 55 minutes. In another district, I was the teacher of record for three full years of students' elementary school reading instruction that occurred in a replacement program. In this district, I taught mixed grade levels for five 90-minute periods per week. Neither position came with a set curriculum, so I had to design my own. This book has come from that work and those teaching experiences and conditions, and the point of explaining that is so that you reader know it is possible to explore Shakespeare with children and reach learning goals regardless of the time related circumstances in which you are teaching.

As you begin your journey exploring Shakespeare with your students these tips may be helpful. First, read through the entire text to gain a bird's-eye view of the unit. With an overall understanding of the unit and its components, as well as an idea of how much time you have to explore Shakespeare, you can begin to make decisions about which learning goals to prioritize and which to eliminate in order to meet the needs of your students given the time you have available.

Because the majority of students do not have significant background knowledge of Shakespeare and his works or of drama in general, direct instruction should take place in brief, but consistently occurring parts of students' exploration throughout their study on an as needed basis. This is why there are many examples of how student learning goals apply to Shakespeare's *A*

*Midsummer Night's Dream*, *Romeo and Juliet*, and *Hamlet* throughout the text. Use these examples for your own reference, as instructional examples in brief mini lessons, or, ideally, as ideas to guide students towards during discussions through questioning techniques. To the greatest degree possible: See what the students can discover on their own first. Let them struggle mightily. Question them to guide them, but avoid giving them answers.

My next tip is this: Stretch or shrink lessons as needed. You have complete permission to rework, adjust, or skip activities that do not work for your class as written. It is perfectly fine to use these activities as springboards or starting points for lessons that do work for your students. Each time I explore Shakespeare with students the lessons and activities vary – no activity is identical each time I have taught it because no group of students is ever identical.

Considering the information related to festival planning way ahead of time will be enormously valuable to your sanity because getting a general sense of what your festival will include as you are making instructional decisions and selecting activities from Chapters 2–8 will allow the festival and instruction to work in tandem.

Finally, think of Chapters 1 and 9 as book ends, and Chapters 2–8 as slim volumes in between. Each volume is its own little book focused on a specific learning goal. You select the volumes that are appropriate for your class, but don't forget to include the book ends or the whole thing collapses! Some form of a Shakespeare Festival that is student planned and executed fuels student motivation to work hard because the reason is within their sights, and the outcome is within their control. This could be as grand as an evening event at school or as modest as the class next door coming to watch a performance and view the projects of their peers.

## Reviewing the Anchor Texts

What, you don't remember *Hamlet*, *Romeo and Juliet*, and *A Midsummer Night's Dream* by heart from your hours spent devoted to your high school English teacher's instruction back when you were 15 or 17? I didn't either when I started. This is not a problem at all. What follows are brief summaries limited to information relevant to the learning activities described in this book. After reading these I suggest reading the Lamb texts and the Shortened Shakespeare texts provided with this book. Finally, after reviewing the media options in Chapter 7, watch a film version of the texts. The *No Fear Shakespeare* series is also an excellent resource for considering the Bard's original language next to a modern translation. You do not have to be a Shakespearean scholar in order to be worthy of exploring the Bard with your students.

## *Hamlet* Summary

*Hamlet* is the story of Prince Hamlet of Denmark whose father has recently been murdered by Claudius, Prince Hamlet's own uncle. To make matters worse, Claudius also marries Prince Hamlet's mother, Gertrude. Hamlet is plagued by visits from his dead father King Hamlet who asks his son to seek revenge against Claudius for his murder. The play sees Hamlet struggle with his ghostly father's demand. Desperate to determine whether the accusation of his father's ghost is true, Hamlet works to find a way to the truth. He thinks he may have found a solution when a group of traveling actors arrives at Elsinore Castle to perform. Hamlet instructs them to perform a play with a similar plot to the events happening in Hamlet's real life. Hamlet's plan is to look to Claudius to see if he reveals any guilty feelings during the performance. Hamlet knows that if Claudius behaves strangely during the play then that is an indication of his guilt. In the meantime, Claudius and Gertrude notice that Hamlet is acting sullen and depressed. Presumably plagued by guilt, the two pressure Hamlet's friends Rosencrantz and Guildenstern to find out what is wrong with Hamlet and report back to them. Polonius, father to Hamlet's friend Ophelia and her brother Laertes, also tries to help Claudius and Gertrude determine the source of Hamlet's poor mood by suggesting that his foul disposition is a result of the end of his relationship with Polonius' daughter Ophelia.

After the play, Hamlet visits his mother, and while he is arguing with her about Claudius and the message of King Hamlet's ghost, Hamlet murders Polonius who was hiding behind a curtain in Gertrude's room so that he could eavesdrop on their conversation. Polonius' son Laertes becomes so angry with Hamlet that he teams up with Claudius to seek revenge upon Hamlet. Their plan ends tragically.

## Hamlet's Characters

The significant characters in Hamlet are as follows:

Hamlet – Prince Hamlet is the deceased King Hamlet's son.
King Hamlet – King Hamlet is Prince Hamlet's father. He appears as a ghost in the play and tells Hamlet that he was killed by Claudius. He also asks Hamlet to avenge his murder by killing Claudius.
Claudius – Claudius is Hamlet's uncle. He presumably murdered King Hamlet and married his wife, Hamlet's mother, Gertrude.
Gertrude – Gertrude is Prince Hamlet's mother who is now married to Claudius.
Polonius – Polonius is Ophelia and Laertes' father. He wants to advance his position in court, so he helps Claudius and Gertrude determine the cause of Hamlet's gloom. Hamlet accidentally kills Polonius.
Laertes – Laertes is Polonius's son and Ophelia's brother who plots with Claudius to kill Hamlet after Hamlet kills his father and shuns his sister.
Ophelia – Ophelia is Laertes' sister and Polonius' daughter who seems to be in love with Hamlet. After Hamlet inexplicably shuns her and kills her father, she becomes unwell and dies in an accident.
Rosencrantz and Guildenstern – Rosencrantz and Guildenstern are childhood friends of Hamlet who are invited to Elsinore to find out the cause of Hamlet's gloom for Gertrude and Claudius.
Horatio and Marcellus – Horatio and Marcellus are friends of Hamlet.

## Romeo and Juliet Summary

*Romeo and Juliet* is the story of two teens with feuding families who fall in love. Romeo and Juliet meet at a masquerade party at Juliet's house that Romeo attends with his friends. Romeo and

Juliet fall in love and decide to get married even though they come to understand that they are from two families at war with each other. Meanwhile, Tybalt, Juliet's cousin, realizes Romeo has snuck into his family party, and later finds Romeo and his friends in the streets of Verona. Tybalt wants to restore his family's honor by fighting Romeo, but instead he fights Romeo's friend Mercutio and kills him. Romeo then kills Tybalt for killing his friend. This is bad news for Romeo, because the Prince banishes him from Verona. This makes Romeo and Juliet very sad because now they cannot be together. To make matters worse, Juliet's parents, who do not know she is already married to Romeo, command her to marry a guy named Paris. Romeo goes off to Mantua, and Juliet meets with the Friar who married them to get help because she does not want to marry Paris. The Friar gives Juliet a potion that will make her sleep and appear to her family like she is dead, but after several hours will allow her to walk up again. The Friar tells Juliet that he will get a message to Romeo to tell him to meet Juliet in her tomb where she will wake up and they can escape together. Unfortunately, the Friar's message does not get to Romeo in time and when Romeo arrives he thinks she is really dead. This leads him to kill himself, which is a tragic mistake, because shortly after Juliet wakes she discovers her friend Romeo is dead, and then decides to kill herself. Eventually the rest of the Montagues and Capulets realize what has happened and they decide to stop fighting because they see that their conflict led to the deaths of their children.

### *Romeo and Juliet's* **Characters**
The most significant characters in Romeo and Juliet are as follows:

Romeo – Romeo, a Montague, is in love with Rosaline who does not love him back. In order to cheer him up, his friends insist he attend a masquerade ball at a Capulet home. There he meets Juliet whom he immediately loves.
Juliet – Juliet, a Capulet, falls in love with Romeo and agrees to marry him.
Tybalt – Tybalt is Juliet's cousin. He murders Romeo's friend Mercutio and then gets murdered by Romeo.

Mercutio – Mercutio is Romeo's friend who is murdered by Tybalt.
Benvolio – Romeo's friend.
Friar Lawrence – Friar Lawrence marries Romeo and Juliet, and helps them after Romeo is banished.
Juliet's Nurse – Juliet's nurse has been her caretaker since she was a small child. The nurse helps facilitate the wedding.
Lord and Lady Montague – Romeo's parents.
Lord and Lady Capulet – Juliet's parents.
Paris – The boy who has Juliet's father's permission to marry her.

### *A Midsummer Night's Dream* Summary

In *A Midsummer Night's Dream* Egeus visits Theseus, the Duke of Athens, because his daughter is being disobedient and he is hoping the duke can help by enforcing a law which requires daughters to obey their father's wishes. Egeus' daughter, Hermia, is in love with Lysander, but her father wants her to marry a boy named Demitrius instead. This is a problem because not only does Hermia love Lysander and not Demetrius, but her friend Helena is in love with Demetrius – the boy her father wants her to marry! Hermia refuses to obey her father, and so the duke tells her she has a few days to make up her mind, but if she still decides to disobey her father then she will either be executed or have to become a nun. Hermia and Lysander decide to run off together through the forest to Lysander's aunt's house. Hermia tells Helena of their plan, and Helena decides to tell Demetrius because she thinks sharing the news of their plan will make him like her. Demetrius runs off after Lysander and Hermia, and Helena follows him into the forest where strange things happen.

Strange events are caused by Puck and his boss, Oberon, who is the king of the fairies. Oberon and the queen of the fairies, Titania, are having a disagreement at the same time that the young friends run off into the forest. Oberon wants to seek revenge on Titania because she will not give him something he wants, so he orders Puck to go find a magical flower that makes a person fall in love with the first thing they see. Oberon also saw the friends arguing in the forest, so he wants Puck to help them with the magical flower as well. Puck finds the flower and stumbles upon the Mechanicals. The Mechanicals are a group of actors who are rehearsing a play in the forest. They intend to enter a contest the Duke is having on his wedding day in which he will select a play to be performed.

Puck selects Bottom from the Mechanicals and transforms him into a donkey who he then places near Titania so that she will see him upon waking. He then finds a couple who he assumes are the friends Oberon wanted him to use the flower on as well. Unfortunately it was not the correct couple, so Puck's actions result in chaos. Oberon finds out about the confusion and sets the situation right. With all of the friends correctly connected – Hermia to Lysander and Helena to Demetrius – they fall asleep. The next morning they are found by Theseus and Hippolyta who insist that all of the couples marry and celebrate on their wedding day. In the end, the Mechanicals perform at the wedding and everyone lives happily ever after.

### *A Midsummer Night Dream's* **Characters**

The most significant characters in *A Midsummer Night's Dream* are as follows.

Theseus – Theseus is the Duke of Athens who is set to marry Hippolyta in three days.
Egeus – Egeus is Hermia's father who wants her to marry Demetrius.
Hermia – Hermia is Egeus' daughter who wants to marry Lysander.
Helena – Helena is Hermia's friend. She is in love with Demetrius, but initially he is not in love with her.
Lysander – Lysander loves Hermia, and she loves him, but her father will not allow them to marry.
Demetrius – Demetrius is supposed to marry Hermia. At the opening of the story Helena is in love with him, but he does not love her.
Bottom – Bottom is a member of the Mechanicals acting troupe. He is transformed by Puck into a donkey whom Titania falls in love with after Puck and Oberon trick her.
Oberon – Oberon is the king of the fairies and Titania's mate.

Titania – Titania is the queen of the fairies and Oberon's mate.
Puck – Puck is a mischievous sprite who works for Oberon.

## Setting the Stage

The following activities provide opportunities for building anticipation as well as background knowledge. They serve as your first steps into Shakespeare with your students.

**Prediction Gallery Walk** – Post artwork inspired by Shakespeare around the class. This can be done with actual printed pictures, or with the help of technology. Without providing much background information, have students rotate through the images making predictions as they do so. You can choose to post artwork inspired by the Shakespearean work that will serve as the anchor text for your student's exploration if you have already chosen for the class, or you can post artwork inspired by all three stories, *A Midsummer Night's Dream*, *Romeo and Juliet*, and *Hamlet*, and use this activity as a means to introducing all three texts to students and letting them select the story that they will study. Chapter 7 provides suggested art for this activity.

**Google Surveys** – Develop a survey related to the story themes using Google Survey or another survey application of your choice that allows you to display results as a graph or chart. Have the class take the survey anonymously and then share and discuss results with the class. Here are some ideas for survey questions related to each anchor text.

*A Midsummer Night's Dream*
- Have you ever had a dream that felt real when you woke up?
- Have you ever been jealous of a friend?
- Has your family ever made what you felt were unfair demands of you?

*Romeo and Juliet*
- Have you ever had a crush on a person?
- Have you ever imagined using violence to solve a problem?
- Have you ever experienced unintended consequences?

*Hamlet*
- Have you ever been disappointed in the way adults behave?
- Have you ever caught another person in a lie or told a lie to protect yourself?
- Have you ever had a feeling that a person you thought was your friend is actually not a good friend at all?

- **Debate** – Debate can be a fantastic way to energize and excite students. Refer to Chapter 6 for a debate lesson that can be used to ignite curiosity in your students as they begin their exploration of Shakespeare. Debating the thematic issues of the anchor text early in their exploration will prime student minds to connect the text to theme as they read.
- **When was Will?** – Create a brief slideshow introduction to Shakespeare's life and times that is based on Bill Bryson's book called *Shakespeare: The World As A Stage* and other resources of your choosing, or search for a free shared presentation available online that sets Shakespeare within the historical context of the Elizabethan Era. There are many available to use, just be sure to check for accuracy. Considering Shakespeare's historical context also primes students to consider what else was going on in the rest of the world which is a favorite independent project for students to share during the Museum portion of the Shakespeare Festival that culminates this learning adventure. For further information about student project ideas please refer to Chapter 9.
- **Direct and Do** – I like teaming direct instruction with an activity that allows kids to apply what they have learned immediately after doing it. Direct instruction on the following topics and terms can help set students up for a successful exploration of Shakespeare by orienting them to information that may be entirely new.
- Language and structure of drama.
    - Direct: Teach students the meanings of these words. Show examples, or have students do an image search for each.

- Cast.
- Act.
- Scene.
- Lines.
- Aside.
- Stage directions.
- Prose.
- Verse.
- Do: Put students into teams of three. Have each team create a script for a one-minute performance. The script must include correct examples of each definition taught. Students may perform their scripts or use them for the Language and Structure of Film Direct and Do.
- Language and structure of film.
  - Direct: Teach students the meanings of these words which are all important to the discussion and ability to compare and contrast multimedia as a secondary text. Show appropriate examples. It is important that the chosen definition include the reason for why such a shot might be used.
  - Camera shots: Wide, medium, close up, and point of view.
  - Camera angles: High and low.
  - Focus.
  - Color.
  - Setting.
  - Costume.
  - Lighting.
  - Sound and music.
  - Performance.
  - Do: Put students into teams of three. Have each team create a one-minute film. The film must include correct examples of each definition taught.

## Resources

The following list of resources can help support and enrich your exploration of Shakespeare with students.

These two slim texts written by historian and humorist Bill Bryson are interesting reads about the evolution of the English language and the life and times of Shakespeare himself.

Bryson, B. (2007). *Shakespeare: The World As A stage.* Atlas Books/HarperPress.

Bryson, B. (1990). *The Mother Tongue: English and How It Got that Way.* William Morrow Paperbacks.

An episode of *Gardener's World* is an excellent and interesting introduction to the plants of *Hamlet* and *A Midsummer Night's Dream*. It is a fun hook to use to inspire student interest prior to making adaptations to botanicals that reflect a student selected setting, reading passages that feature botanicals prominently, discussing the central conflicts and how they are resolved – with plant-based potions and poisons, or doing any of the plant related activities in this resource.

Rawlings, C (Producer). (2016). *Shakespeare's Plant Potions and Poisons* (2016, episode 7). Proto, P. (Executive producer). *Gardeners' World.* BBC Two. https://www.bbc.co.uk/programmes/p03rvqv9

Myshakespeare provides interactive versions of Shakespeare's works that feature video clips, visuals, and explanations via links within the text.

*Myshakespeare*. (2023, May 31). https://myshakespeare.com/

The Folger Shakespeare Library provides an abundance of articles, resources, lessons, and media related to understanding and teaching Shakespeare.

*Teach*. (2023, May 31). Folger Shakespeare Library. https://www.folger.edu/teach/

The infamous Shakespeare insult generator can be found here:

*Shakespearean insults generator!* (n.d.). Shakespearean Insults Generator. https://www.literarygenius.info/a1-shakespearean-insults-generator.htm

Brendan Kelso's revisions of Shakespeare's work transforms the plays into 10-minute romps that feature about 10–20% of Shakespeare's language and 80–90% modern language.

*Shakespeare for Kids: The best Shakespeare for Kids Books & Plays*. Shakespeare for Kids Books. (2023, June 6). https://playingwithplays.com/

## References

Buchmann, M., & Steinhoff, A. (2017). Co-development of student agency components and its impact on educational attainment—Theoretical and methodological considerations. *Research in Human Development, 14*(2), 96–105. https://doi.org/10.1080/15427609.2017.1305818

Fisher, D. (2012). Text dependent questions. *Principal Leadership*, 70–73.

Fisher, D., & Frey, N. (2012). Close reading in elementary classrooms. *The Reading Teacher, 66*(3), 179–188.

Fisher, D., Frey, N., & Hattie, J. (2016). *Visible learning for literacy, grades K-12: Implementing the practices that work best to accelerate student learning*. Corwin Press.

Johnston, P.H. (2004). *Choice words: How our language affects children's learning*. Stenhouse Publishers.

Kerr, R., & Booth, B. (1978). Specific and varied practice of motor skill. *Perceptual and Motor Skills, 46*(2), 395–401.

Lamb, C., & Lamb, M. (1807). *Tales from Shakespeare*. Juvenile Library of William Godwin.

Meta, J., & Fine, S. (2019). *In search of deeper learning*. Harvard University Press.

Otis, N., Grouzet, F.M.E., & Pelletier, L.G. (2005). Latent motivational change in an academic setting: A 3-year longitudinal study. *Journal of Educational Psychology, 97*(2), 170–183.

Pearson, P.D., & Johnson, D.D. (1978). *Teaching reading comprehension*. Holt, Rinehart & Winston.

Shakespeare, W. (1596). *A midsummer night's dream*.

Shakespeare, W. (1597). *Romeo and Juliet*.

Shakespeare, W. (1601). *Hamlet*.

Shawer, S.F. (2010). Classroom-level curriculum development: EFL Teachers as curriculum-developers, curriculum-makers and curriculum-transmitters. *Teaching and Teacher Education, 26*, 173–180.

Tomlinson, C.A. (2005). *How to differentiate instruction in mixed ability classrooms*. ASCD.

Wang, M. T., & Eccles, J. (2011). Adolescent behavioral, emotional, and cognitive engagement trajectories in school and their differential relations to educational success. *Journal of Research on Adolescence*, *22*(1), 31–33.

Wigfield, A., Eccles, J. S., Fredricks, J. A., Simpkins, S., Roeser, R. W., & Schiefele, U. (2015). *Handbook of child psychology and developmental science*. John Wiley & Sons, Inc.

Wiggins, G., & McTighe, J. (2008). *Understanding by design*. ASCD.

# 2
# Questioning, Annotating, and Answering to Comprehend

This chapter is focused on learning goals that require students to make sense of the text through asking and answering questions before, during, and after reading, by making inferences, and through using text evidence to support such inferences. Wow. That sounds riveting. Kids are about as excited to come near that type of learning activity as I am to whatever is now inside of the bowl that was once leftover soup at the back of my fridge. That is, unless they are answering questions that come from their own thinking and their peers' thinking. Like tidying up the congealing stock in my fridge is best for my health, so too is asking and answering questions about the health of a student's understanding of a text. But when those questions come from the teacher, rather than themselves, it's as appetizing as me offering you a bowl of soup made from the infamous stock. This module centers on a close reading routine that sets the stage for healthy comprehension based on student rather than teacher led inquiry.

Close reading at its best puts student questions first and reminds me of how I met my best friend of nearly 40 years, Holly. She first found me precariously balanced on a discarded bin, face deep in a dumpster down the alley from our houses. I was diving for the art supplies I had spotted while riding my bike. Boxes and bags and cases and mysterious tins were scattered around me. There was a treasure trove of goodies: Markers and stickers and fancy papers. Holly joined right in on the hunt. Now. Had our mothers told us to go play in the garbage down the alley we would have thought it a ridiculous idea, but because we found it on our own the dump had the cachet of a boutique art supply shop. We can create that same feeling of anticipation and discovery for our students if we allow them to treasure hunt through the text for their own prizes. Let Shakespeare be a dumpster overflowing with opportunity for your kids. Those opportunities come in the form of questions and inferences that they will share. In my experience, the routines listed in this chapter allow students to do just that while also building comprehension. For this reason, I don't take that treasure hunt moment away from the kids by doing too much explicit teaching of specific questions. Rather, I give as much control as possible to the students. So, when a student hands me what may be a gem of a question encased in doubt and confusion, I may help them excavate the idea, but the idea originates with them.

> So, when a student hands me what may be a gem of a question encased in doubt and confusion, I may help them excavate the idea, but the idea originates with them.

This close read routine includes three readings distinguished by their purpose and length of time. The routine is completed over six class sessions. The first reading occurs over three sessions and focuses on basic comprehension as well as asking and answering text dependent questions (TDQs) as a group. As the routine progresses, there is a gradual release of responsibility to students, and as students progress with the readings their questioning should continue to evolve in complexity. The second reading is done in partnerships and involves answering TDQs over two days, while the final reading is done independently and is an opportunity to stage tableaus and informally assess students abilities to ask and answer questions.

## Close Reading Round One

Close reading routines in my classroom begin with students gathering together with pencils and highlighters and sticky notes as I pass out the text. At this point, I have already left them with cliffhanger comments that capture their curiosity such as, "This story is going to leave you wondering how we can manage to stage a sword fight in school" (*Romeo and Juliet*). Or, "Who believes in ghosts?" (*Hamlet*). And, "What is the worst thing that a friend can do to you?" (*A Midsummer Night's Dream*). Students know that the first reading is when we get to interrogate the author by pointing out all of the things that do not make sense to us. This strategy helps students become more comfortable sharing their questions because the "fault" for their struggles with comprehension becomes reframed as the author's issue and not their own. As I read to model fluency, the students furiously scribble questions in the margins or highlight text to interrogate until they get to the question that summarizes their confusion. When I pause, hands shoot up. The students want to share the questions they have for our author.

If only it went like that all the time. From time to time students struggle, so when I see that during the first reading students are engaged and able to jot down question annotations within my pauses, then I allow them to clip along without intervention. However, when I see a sea of agonized and lost faces, I switch to a more interactive approach, pausing and not only waiting quietly, but noticing who might be able to support their classmates through conversation. When I see the kids are really struggling I pivot to a more shared approach and incorporate a think aloud.

There will be pitfalls: Students may be too shy or resistant to share their questions. In this case, model more, and give lots of time. Students may need practice asking questions first through a game, so try playing the Question Game (located at the end of the chapter). Scaffold from what students do know. When we hand children the insights or learning they are supposed to take away from the lessons(s), we may be operating with more efficiency, which seems like a good idea because we have so much content to "get through," but until we learn that we must go slow to go fast, and give the kids the time to process, our work will be in vain because we have not allowed for learning to take place. Keep in mind that the beauty of teaching Shakespeare is that you will struggle through the meaning making together and there is magic in that. Struggle with the kids. It's OK.

At the conclusion of the day's reading students sort questions into three piles. Our other close read helper, QAR strategy, tells us that different question types need different types of answers. Those that require inferential evidence and those that require explicit evidence, both considered TDQs, make two of the piles, and the third pile is for those questions that do not require the text to be answered at all. My students call that third group "wonderers" (W). Wonderers are questions that require further research, or even just one's imagination or personal experience to answer. Students sort questions into one of the three piles by analyzing the question and looking in the text for answers. If the question can be answered directly from the text – it's an explicit question and the answer requires text evidence. If the question needs the text and our own thinking and explanation then the question is inferential. And, if the question can be answered without looking in the focus text at all, or needs other research, it's a wonderer. Sorted questions are displayed on posters of question types and the ingredients needed to answer them for student reference. At this point, as a class, we work through an example of how to answer each type of text dependent question by using the Critical Thinking: Questioning and Answering document.

This process repeats over the course of three days. During day one students complete this routine with the beginning third of the text. On day two the focus is on the middle third, and on day three the final third. It is also possible to use the tildes, those funny little squiggles that look like this ~, throughout the Lamb texts to organize the three days of close reading according to Acts. For instance, day one may focus on Acts 1 and 2, day two on Acts 3 and 4, and day three on Act 5.

## Close Reading Round Two

The close reading routine picks up pace with the second round because students are now familiar with the text. At this point the focus shifts from addressing a mix of implicit and explicit questions to mostly working with implicit questions as they are more rigorous. Also, during the second round of reading, the focus narrows to a more specific purpose. This purpose will arise from either posted student questions, by the teacher who has reflected on student needs and chosen a path of instructional planning to meet those needs. For example, in a classroom in which the teacher has decided to focus on character, and specifically how a character's decisions affect the plot, then a more meaningful round two reading would be to ask students to annotate with a "C" anywhere they notice a character making a choice, and an "O" anywhere the reader can identify an outcome of that choice to assist them in answering the question: Do the outcomes of character's choices serve their best interests? Through discussion, this question might also be excavated from a student question that was originally written like this: "Is marrying Romeo even a good idea?"

Another difference from the first round of reading is that in this second reading students read the text aloud within a small group and they also annotate together. This allows students to practice fluency which will be important as they perform later in their exploration of Shakespeare. After students complete the second reading, they can work together to answer the focus question using the Critical Thinking: Questioning and Answering document.

## Close Read Round Three

The third close reading follows the same process as round one, except students complete their reading and writing independently to demonstrate their ability to ask and answer a question as they read. For this round students might focus on the entire text, or a specific act or passage. Again, they read to annotate text that will help them answer a specific set of questions that include at least one inferential and one explicit question. The questions in this round should come from the students themselves.

In addition, during the final reading, groups of students focus on a specific act to determine the most pivotal scene. That scene will be the focus of a tableau to be staged as a culminating activity for this module. A tableau is a frozen scene. Imagine that you are watching your favorite action movie, and you pause at a critical point in the film. The characters, just previously animated by a battle scene or argument, are now still, as if in a photograph. This is a tableau, and creating a tableau is an opportunity for students to practice identifying pivotal scenes in the plot and performing Shakespeare. Further, since they are looking for a scene that contains multiple characters involved in dramatic action that is also a pivotal point in the plot, they are practicing the higher level skill of evaluating. As students take their ideas to small groups to decide they are also doing verbally what they have been doing in written form – stating a claim and providing reasoning and evidence to support their claim. In this case, the claim is which scene would make the best tableau and their reasoning would be based on the scene's meeting the criteria for a tableau. Staging tableaux are the highlight of this module as it gives the students a hint of the thrill that comes from performing.

## Close Reading with Shakespeare

The first days of exploring Shakespeare with middle-grade students, in my experience, are best spent with Mary and Charles Lamb, so the close reading lessons in this chapter are based on their adapted version of *A Midsummer Night's Dream*, *Romeo and Juliet*, and *Hamlet* from their 1856 collection called *Tales of Shakespeare*. That said, should you find the content too facile for your students another option for the close reading could be the Shortened Shakespeare. If you think your students are ready to jump right in, then by all means – do so!

I advise selecting two stories. This will give students a choice of stories to perform, and focusing on two stories will provide excellent compare and contrast opportunities as outlined in Chapter 8. Any two of the stories that are highlighted in this resource – *Hamlet*, *Romeo and Juliet*, or *A Midsummer Night's Dream* – will pair well for such a purpose. It is not necessary to study all three, though reading two is optimal if your goal is to compare Shakespeare's works. Choose based on what learning goals you have in mind for your students and what you can accomplish in the time available.

The purpose of the activities in this module is to attain basic comprehension of the stories so that with subsequent experiences of the text the students can take their understanding to deeper levels. During the close reading of the stories is not the time to tackle every single comprehension issue. The key is the gist – do the kids have a general sense of the plot? Can they find text to help them answer their questions as they read? If so, mission accomplished. The goal at this point is not to understand the finer points of anything. Each subsequent chapter of this resource will offer lessons for going deeper: Character analysis, vocabulary acquisition, comparing and contrasting, etc. but at this point the goal is to just understand the basic plot. I have found basic comprehension is the biggest hurdle educators perceive when considering approaching the bard with students. In my experience, close reads organized around student questions have been a successful tool to surmounting that challenge.

## Learning Goals

The learning goals for this chapter are related to asking questions, and answering them by making claims, and supporting claims with text evidence. This process serves as comprehension development. The initial level requires that students provide text evidence. This might come in the form of a summary or paraphrase rather than a direct quote. As students progress through the skills, the next level requires that the student directly quote their evidence from the text. At subsequent levels, students progress to making multiple citations. Finally, students work to evaluate, and select the best text evidence for their claim from a pool of possible evidence.

Stating learning goals directly will help students identify the purpose of instruction and thus be more likely to achieve it. Specifically, students will be able to ask and answer comprehension questions by using text evidence to support their thinking and claims. This can be stated as follows for students: I can ask questions to help me become curious about what I am reading. And, I can use text evidence to answer questions that I or others develop.

## Module Learning Goals

| | Going Far | | | | |
|---|---|---|---|---|---|
| | 4 | 5 | 6 | 7 | 8 |
| Evidence | Shared Evidence to support their claim. | Quoted evidence to support their claim. | Cited one piece of evidence to support their claim. | Cited several pieces of evidence to support their claim. | Cited several pieces of best evidence to support their claim. |
| | Going Deep | | | | |
| Inference | ____My answers to text dependent questions included inferences I made and supported. | | | | |
| Explanation | ____When my answers included an inference, I thoroughly explained how my evidence supported my inference. | | | | |
| Questioning | ____I asked questions at all three levels. ____My questions helped reach a deeper level of comprehension. | | | | |

The benchmarks for this learning goal were established using the Common Core Standards.

## Assessments

Learning goals in this module can be assessed in multiple ways. First, a pre-assessment option would be to pose a text dependent question on a Critical Thinking: Questioning and Answering document regarding paragraph one of the appropriate Lamb anchor text prior to beginning the close read routine. Next, using the results of the pre-assessment, have students complete a self-assessment and plan for their learning using the rubric for this module as a guide for goal setting. Have students reflect on their desired level of performance, and chart them on the assessment rubric for this chapter. Finally, at the end of the module, conduct a traditional assessment using student generated questions and a Critical Thinking: Questioning and Answering document. Or, ask the same question posed in the pre-assessment and have students generate a response after studying the text. Lastly, have students return to their goal setting and reflect.

## Activities

The Critical Thinking: Questioning and Answering document is an online editable resource available for this lesson.

## Critical Thinking: Questioning and Answering

Scholar's Name _____

Text Dependent Question

_____

_____

| | **Explicit TDQ Thin Question** The answer comes directly from the text. The answer might be in one spot or multiple spots. | | **Implicit TDQ Thick Question** The answer comes from our inference. Text evidence is needed to support our thinking. |
|---|---|---|---|
| | | **Create a claim by restating the question and including the answer.** | |
| | | **Provide text evidence.** | |
| | | **Explain how each piece of text evidence supports your claim.** | |

Copyright material from Jennifer Szwaya (2024), *Shakespeare Amazes in the Classroom*, Routledge

The Three-Panel Comic Strip is also an online editable resource available for this lesson.

## Three-Panel Comic

Scholar's Name _____

## Close Reading Routine – First Reading – Three 45-to-60-minute Sessions

1. Establish the purpose of reading.

*The purpose of reading the text this first time is to gain an understanding of the plot events. If we are going to be performing the stories, we must certainly understand them first. When we are done reading we want to be able to retell what happened, so as we read we need to be listening for who the characters are and what problems those characters are facing. As we read we want to identify the parts of the text we do not understand or that we have a question about by highlighting it. We also want to highlight newer vocabulary. I will read to model fluent reading and because our listening comprehension is stronger than our reading comprehension. As I read, you will highlight new or unfamiliar words, and annotate with a question mark next to text that is unclear or which you have a question about. I will pause from time to time to let you write out your specific questions. Your questions may have answers in the text or may be questions that require inferences. Let's dig into this dumpster, interview Shakespeare's work, and see what treasures we can find!*

2. Read the text aloud, pausing at appropriate intervals to allow students to annotate questions that correspond to passages they may have highlighted. Use these pauses to make the read aloud interactive and/or shared, depending on the needs of the class.

Students gather with the text, a pencil, and a highlighter. The teacher will read the text at a slower pace to model fluency, so that students can focus on listening to make meaning and jotting questions. As the teacher reads, they should direct students to jot a question mark in an area of text that leaves them unclear or wondering something. Pause at the end or middle and end of each page to allow students to go back and write out their specific question. This process will need to be modeled several times before the students settle into the routine successfully.

If the students are not able to annotate with a question, you may have them start by highlighting challenging passages as you read. As you can imagine, this leads to a lot of highlighter use. However, students highlighting difficult passages teamed with a shared reading approach can be effective tools as the following conversation demonstrates.

*Teacher*: (Looking out over a sea of neon pages after reading paragraphs one to four of A Midsummer Night's Dream.) Did anyone highlight anything that was confusing or unclear?
*Class*: (Groaning, complaining, and all raising hands or completely frozen in fear.)
*Teacher*: (Thinking this might be a good time to switch to a shared reading approach in which she models identifying tricky passages and asking questions to better understand, decides to wait.)
*Student*: Yes, I highlighted all of paragraph one.
*Teacher*: Interesting. Why?
*Student*: I just don't get it.
*Teacher*: Yes, this is challenging. Let's change things up. What do you get?
*Student*: Nothing.
*Teacher*: You must get something. Even if it's super tiny. What is one tiny thing you did understand?
*Student*: Well, I did get that Egeus is a dad.
*Teacher*: Great! Can anyone else add to that?
*Student 2*: Yes. I get that he does not want to let his daughter marry someone.
*Teacher*: Good. Does this make anyone think of specific questions?
*Student 3*: Who does Egeus not want his daughter to marry? Why?
*Student 4*: Who is Theseus?
*Student 5*: Why doesn't his daughter want to marry that one guy?

It is possible to scaffold the skill of asking questions by asking students to share passages that they thought were confusing, and then simply asking, what makes this passage confusing? What questions do we have about this passage? If, these questions teamed with ample wait time do not continue the conversations with students doing the majority of the thinking, then switching to a shared reading approach in which the teacher projects the text, specifically identifies a confusing passage, and models identifying questions may be more appropriate until the students grow more successful independently.

By days two and three of the first reading students should be more comfortable developing questions, but remember, we want them to go dumpster diving, we do not want them to stand outside the dumpster while we, the teacher, get to jump in and hand them insights. Students should be empowered to make their own inquiries and discoveries. Try to give them less and allow them to struggle more. Productive struggle is the idea that in order to make gains in learning whether it is Math, tennis, or Shakespeare, students need to struggle in order to grow (Kerr & Booth, 1978). The students need to get comfortable generating the questions. This will be a test of your patience. Your wait time will be stretched like never before, but the kids need to know that you are serious about them being the ones to dive into the text – to make meaning. We want to cultivate a curiosity so that students go looking for meaning on their own. This is a transferable skill that will serve them beyond this study of Shakespeare.

3. After reading the day's selection, recap the reading together perhaps with a "Yes, and…" circle, and then ask students to share examples of their questions. In a "Yes, and…" circle, students share with one small adjustment. They first acknowledge the previous student's comment by saying, "yes, such and so and so did…" which recaps the last student's share, and is followed by an "and…" that includes the current student's comments (Leonard & Yorton, 2015). As students share, ask them to identify the questions by their type, and sort onto question type posters to model the sorting activity they will be doing next. As they do, invite the class to share their answers or thinking to the TDQs. Using the Critical Thinking: Questioning and Answering document, model how to answer a text only and a text and inference type question. This will allow for the most important

clarifications to be made. As students share their thinking about the answers, be sure to ask, or have students ask each other to locate the text evidence that supports their thinking. In order to best develop student agency, the teacher may opt to choose several student question examples, so that students have a choice regarding which question they answer.

For the text and inference type example, choose a fairly straightforward example. This will help give your lesson momentum because students will anticipate answering the more complex questions if you label them as such and promise to come back to them. To maximize anticipation, discuss questions such as this, but then leave the question unanswered and your findings inconclusive. Terminate the conversation on a cliffhanger.

During days two and three of the first read, if students struggled on day one use this time to model further, or add the Critical Thinking: Questioning and Answering document time after the question sort. Allow teams to choose one of each question type to answer in partnerships or small groups. This will also free you to model within smaller groups, if necessary.

4. After identifying and answering several examples each question type, dismiss students to each record five of their questions on sticky notes, and within groups have the students sort the selected questions onto the correct question type poster.

An important piece of the first reading routine is the question sort. As the annotating and read aloud portion of the day is complete, sit with the students beginning at the start of the day's selection of text, and have the students share their questions. Not all questions will get answered, nor should they, and that is OK. The point is to resolve some of their more basic plot comprehension questions shared among the group and get a sense of where their comprehension may be failing. As students share questions, ask the class to think about show each question should be categorized. Model via think aloud how you would categorize the question into these groups.

Posters of titled question groupings should be posted in the room. The teacher may have the class rotate to review each of the question posters to ensure that they were categorized correctly. Another option would be to check the categories after class and have the students reclassify those that were wrong the following day. Yet another option would be classifying questions as a class after students read them aloud. On day one the teacher should select one of the text-based and inference-based questions to model answering for the group. This can be done using the Critical Thinking: Questioning and Answering document which can be found in the online resources. This example can serve as a model for students to refer to as they answer on their own during upcoming sessions. On subsequent days students should complete this activity in groups, partnerships, and then individually before being assessed formally.

5. Students complete one panel of the three-panel comic strip as they finish the sort.

    At the conclusion of each day's readings, have students complete one frame on the comic strip panels, so that by the end of the second readings they have a mini comic strip of the entire story. This strategy will help solidify their comprehension of main plot events. There are lots of adventuress to take with the comic strips as well. For instance, students might choose to retell one story arc rather than the general story, then these comics can be cut into their individual panels. Students can then create a larger comic integrating the various arcs. A simple three-panel strip however will help them identify the main plot arc. Student comics can be cut apart and combined to make more detailed plot arcs. The student work pictured gives an example of two comics that might be cut apart and recombined to create a more complex comic or plot arc.

## Second Reading: Two 45–60 Minute Sessions

1. Set the purpose for the second reading by posing several options for the students from the text and inference board. Discuss with the students how we might hunt for evidence as we do our second readings.

*The purpose of the second reading is to deeply analyze the text through the lens of your own questions. This is the portion of the close read in which you will begin to see the power you have in making meaning of what you read. You do not always need a teacher to tell you what things mean. Through your own questions and through the power of hunting for text evidence and reflecting on meaning – you can figure things out for yourself. Shakespeare's stories are great places to practice the skills of being a good reader, but know that asking and answering questions as you read will be a skill that you will use over and over in life.*

In preparation, read through the questions that students sorted into the inference and text pile. From these questions select two or three that are particularly interesting. Then have students read in partnerships while annotating text. Alternately, have student partnerships select their own focus questions. Student engagement tends to be higher when those messy questions, the questions that the class may have discussed a bit earlier and then put to the side for later at a cliff hanger moment in the conversation, are reintroduced to students. The second reading is an excellent opportunity to practice fluency, while also seeking text evidence to support thinking.

2. Pair students to complete the second reading. As they read, they will do so aloud, annotating as they do. Annotations will differ with each question.

The reason for annotations being dependent on the question is because we want the students to be using the strategy of annotating to find text evidence, therefore, the annotation must be specific to the question. For instance, a point of confusion in *Romeo and Juliet* is related to the miscommunications among the characters. At some point, students wonder how it came to be that Romeo thought Juliet was dead when he arrived back in Verona. How did he not know his *wife* was faking it? Asking students to reread with the focus being on which character knows what when can allow a student to clarify their own understanding if they annotate points in the story when someone learns new information with an "N." Due to the lengthy monologues, a great deal of confusion about *Hamlet* is expressed by the question: What is happening here? So, rereading with the purpose of annotating with an ST for self-talk when a character is speaking to themselves can help a student see the overall structure of the work, and better understand it as a whole.

3. Student pairs discuss the evidence gathered and consider what the answer to their question may be. They should also evaluate their annotations to determine which evidence best answers the question and, if necessary, supports their inference.

Depending on group size, select three-to-five questions with the class to address in this activity, and divide the class into the same number of home teams. Next, assign, or have team members select which questions they will answer. Then, have the teams reorganize themselves into question groups so that all students working on the same question are in a group rather than with their home team. When students each complete a Critical Thinking: Questioning and Answering sheet for their question with their question team, have the students reorganize into the home teams which will now have a member who has completed one of each of the questions. Home teams should take turns sharing their findings as the rest of the team evaluates their thinking and evidence selection. Critical Thinking: Questioning and Answering documents can be found in the online resources.

4. Student teams complete a Critical Thinking: Questioning and Answering document for their question.
5. If the second reading is being completed with a variety of questions, then teams should share their question and findings with the class, to enhance overall comprehension.

### Third Reading: One 45–60 Minute Session
1. Students read independently. As they read, they are doing so for several purposes.

*The purpose for today's reading is for you to read independently. While you read, you will be annotating text to help you answer a text dependent question. Finally, you will be reading to select the scene most significant to plot development for our tableaux.*

2. Students independently complete a Critical Thinking: Questioning and Answering document to demonstrate their ability to use text evidence and reasoning to answer an inferential question. The questions students are annotating to answer can be directly assigned by the teacher, or be students selected from a pool of options.
3. After the independent informal assessment, students join teams, and within their teams, students should come to consensus regarding which scene in the story to base their tableau. I advise assigning text to students based on acts so that the groups were not all making their choices from the same area of text. It is preferable that teams be separated while they practice staging their tableaux.
4. Finally, tableaus are photographed and shared.

Photographs can be projected during a class discussion in which students make a case for which scene is being portrayed. Photographs can also be printed for such an activity to be done as an independent or small group activity. A further activity could require students to put the photos in chronological order and argue their position using text evidence.

**FIGURE 2.1** Students create a tableau as they rehearse *Romeo and Juliet*.

Note: In this chapter, an engraving of Shakespeare's face by Charles Droeshout (1623) has been used to protect children's identities in photographs.

## Learning Tools

These are examples of the types of questions that students tend to ask. Questions in regular font can be answered correctly directly from the text, while italicized questions require an inference or opinion and supporting text evidence to be answered well. Finally, questions in bold are more wondering questions and can be answered with an opinion, the imagination, or with the help of other other texts and sources.

## Close Reading of *A Midsummer Night's Dream* Tools

### Paragraphs 1–18
*Act 1*

What does the law of Athens allow its citizens to do?
*Is this law of Athens fair?*
*Do you think Egeus is a mean dad? Why or why not?*
Who is in love with who in this story? Explain the relationships between Lysander, Demetrius, Helena, and Hermia.
*Why do you think Helena tells Demetrius about Hermia and Lysander running away?*

Questioning, Annotating, and Answering ◆ 45

*Is Helena a better friend to Hermia, or is Hermia a better friend to Helena?*
Why is Oberon jealous of Titania?
Who is Puck?
Why does Oberon want a flower?
What did Puck see when he was getting the flower?

## Paragraphs 19–33
*Acts 2 and 3*

What other job does Oberon give Puck?
What jobs do Titania's fairies do while she sleeps?
*How well did Puck follow Oberon's directions?*
Why are Hermia and Helena fighting?

## Paragraphs 34–65
*Acts 4 and 5*

What is Oberon's plan to fix the confusion caused by the love potions?
Who does Titania fall in love with?
How is the quarrel between Titania and Oberon resolved?
*Do you think Titania should have given Oberon the boy?*

# Close Reading of *Romeo and Juliet* Tools

## Paragraphs 1–8
*Act 1*

*How is the relationship between the Montagues and the Capulets?*
Who is going to the Capulets' supper and why?
Who is Benvolio? Mercutio?
Who is Tybalt and why is he raging?
What do Romeo and Juliet each realize by the end of the supper?
*Why does Romeo want to be a glove?*
*What is Juliet talking about in paragraph four?*
What plan to Romeo and Juliet develop? What does Romeo want from Friar Lawrence?

### Paragraphs 9–17
*Acts 2 and 3*

What happens between Romeo, Mercutio, and Tybalt?
What does the Prince decide?
*How does Juliet feel about the events on the street?*
What does Romeo want when he returns to the Friar?
What new plan do Romeo and Friar Lawrence decide upon?
*Why does her father terrify Juliet?*
Why does Juliet visit the Friar?
What plan do Juliet and the Friar create?
Why is Juliet worried?

### Paragraphs 18–26
*Acts 4 and 5*

What does Paris see when he arrives to wake Juliet?
What news do the messengers bring?
Why does Romeo visit the apothecary?
Why is Paris in the churchyard?
What happens to Paris?
Why does Friar Lawrence have a pickaxe and lantern?
How is Juliet alive?
**Was the fighting worth it?**
**How can we fix hate?**


## Close Reading of *Hamlet* Tools

### Paragraphs 1–11
*Act 1*

Who is Gertrude?
*Is Gertrude a good queen?*
Who is Claudius?
How many Hamlets are in this story?
What happened to King Hamlet?
*What does Prince Hamlet think of his dad?*
What do the soldiers see?

*How does Hamlet feel when he sees the spirit?*
What does the spirit tell Hamlet?
*What effect does seeing the spirit have on Hamlet?*
**Are ghosts real?**

## Paragraphs 12–23
*Acts 2 and 3*

Who is Ophelia?
What does Hamlet tell her in the letter?
*Does Hamlet love Ophelia?*
What happens when Hamlet meets the actors?
Why does Hamlet want the players to perform the story of the murder in Vienna?
**Does theater or art really teach lessons?**
How did Claudius react to the play?
How does Polonius die?
What does Hamlet say to his mother?
*Do you think Hamlet and his mom have a good relationship?*

## Paragraphs 24–27
*Acts 4 and 5*

What is Claudius' plan?
Is Claudius' plan successful?
What happened to Ophelia?
What is Claudius' new plan?
*Do you think Claudius' new plan is successful?*
**Is revenge worth it?**

# Considerations: Including Diverse Learners

Twice exceptional students and multilingual learners might benefit from the following strategies and resources.

## Question Game

The purpose behind the Question Game is to provide question starters to students to help them generate questions. Students will need a set of question cards and a set of word cards. Each set should be color coded so that they can be quickly sorted. Question cards should be labeled: "Who," "What," "When," "Where," "Why," and "How" on the front, and one through six on the back. Word cards should be labeled with the words: "Is," "Are," "Did," "Does," "Can," and "Can't" on the front and with the numbers one through six on the back. Students roll a dice and pick the corresponding number card from the question cards. Then students roll again and pick the corresponding word card. Then they work to generate questions that start with the words on the selected cards. For instance, a student might roll to select how and is. They now try to generate questions that begin with the words "How is…" Examples might include: How is Hamlet affected by his father's death? How is Romeo feeling about Rosaline when he enters the Capulets' party? How is Hermia feeling after Helena speaks? There are endless variations on this strategy such as adding more cards or categories of cards.

## Recordings

Another reason for selecting the Mary and Charles Lamb renditions of Shakespeare's works to start is that there are free recordings of the text available, which can be particularly helpful for twice exceptional students and multilingual learners. The site librivox.com and others provide free audio recordings of works in the public domain.

## Revisiting Essential Unit Question

### What is the power of language?

One of the main ideas that students should be guided to see is that language changes over time. Even with the choice to maintain Shakespeare's vocabulary, Mary and Charles Lamb's stories are visibly different from Shakespeare's, and students will surely recognize immediately how different their own spoken language differs from the Lambs' and from Shakespeare's. Projecting a piece of Shakespeare's text next to the corresponding portion of a Lamb story and then followed by a piece of recent student writing can lead to a fruitful conversation. Add all reasonable ideas to the Shakespeare web as discussed in Chapter 1. Over the years the ideas that consistently emerge from students during this discussion is the fact that the sentences written in 1856 were longer and more complex. Students notice that the form of entertainment changed from drama and poetry to prose. Later, when looking at multimedia and seeing the interpretations of Shakespeare's stories in modern cinema extends this idea that the language of entertainment, and thus language, changes over time. Lastly, students recognize that descriptions in Shakespeare and the Lambs' time were more detailed. This noticing has led to conversations about why that might be, and whether that is a good thing or not.

## Resources

This resource provides a concise overview of close reading.

Jones, B., Chang, S., Heritage, M., Tobiason, G., & Herman, J. (2015). *Supporting students in close reading.* UCLA. National Center for Research on Evaluation, Standards, and Student Testing (CRESST).

This resource provides a concise summary of what text dependent questions are, how they can be used in the classroom, and why they are effective.

Fisher, D., & Frey, N. (2012). Text-dependent questions. *Principal Leadership*, 70–71.

This is the original Lamb text which provides shortened narrative versions of Shakespeare's stories.

Lamb, C., Lamb, M., & Shakespeare, W. (1856). *Tales from Shakespeare.* Phillips, Sampson, and Company.

## References

Kerr, R., & Booth, B. (1978). Specific and varied practice of motor skill. *Perceptual and motor skills*, *46*(2), 395–401. https://doi.org/10.1177/003151257804600201

Leonard, K., & Yorton, T. (2015). *Yes, and: How improvisation reverses "no, but" thinking and improves creativity and collaboration: Lessons from the second city.* Harper Business.

Lamb, C., & Lamb, M. (1807). *Tales from Shakespeare*. Juvenile Library of William Godwin.

National Governors Association Center for Best Practices & Council of Chief State School Officers. (2010). *Common core state standards for English language arts and literacy in history/social studies, science, and technical subjects*. Authors.

Shakespeare, W. (1596). *A midsummer night's dream*.

Shakespeare, W. (1597). *Romeo and Juliet*.

Shakespeare, W. (1601). *Hamlet*.

# 3

# Elements of the Story

## Plot, Character, Setting

Over the course of my years in the classroom, I have found one question to be more important in making lessons relevant to students than any other. This magic question is, "Today, what would you like to be when you grow up?" The magic comes not from asking the question, but from going a step further to apply what was learned about students to classroom lessons during discussions. This is how I persuade students that learning how to state a claim and support it with evidence is worth their time and attention. In fact, I challenge students to stump me with a career interest in which their practice in answering text dependent questions would *not* be useful. Here is an example of how such conversations tend to go.

> The magic comes not from asking the question, but from going a step further to apply what was learned about students to classroom lessons during discussions.

*T:* Okay, kiddos. Today is… a written response day! TDQ (text dependent question) time!
*Students: (Good natured eyerolls and groans.)*
*T:* Seriously though. Who cares? Who cares about doing this? Why should we even care?

DOI: 10.4324/9781003361107-3

*Students:* (*Depending on the mood of the class they may answer this question on their own because we have been through answering it so many times, or they may want some examples from me to help them turn their writing engines over when they need a spark.*)

*T:* Okay, Let's do this. Someone, stump me. If you were to become grown today – what job would you want to be doing? And, how would answering TDQs today help you in that job or situation?

*Student:* Ronaldo! I don't need to write because I am going to be a soccer star!

*T:* Haha! Not so fast! As the team captain Ronaldo is responsible for supporting his team with good plays. If Ronaldo has an idea for how to get past the offense and score a goal, his idea is a claim. He must persuade his coaches and his teammates that his idea for how the play should be run by using reasoning and evidence.

*S:* Ooooh, yeah!

*T:* One more time. Anyone else? Can you stump me?

*S:* I want to be a veterinarian.

*T:* (*Rolling her eyes.*) That is *sooo* easy. I bring my sick dog King Leonidas of Sparta into your vet clinic. You consider his symptoms and you reflect on the medical research you know concerning such symptoms. You decide on a treatment plan – this plan is your claim. Now, you must use evidence and reasoning to persuade me to agree to the treatment plan you developed.

In relating classroom work to the world outside of the classroom and to the student's futures, agency and engagement increase because students see the relevance of what is being taught or asked of them. Taking the time to make the purpose of classroom work clear and relevant is worthwhile because it pays enormous dividends in terms of student investment. Story element lessons are not immediately inspiring, but they can be if we relate such lessons to their future and to life outside the classroom. How can this be accomplished while teaching character, theme, and setting?

Let's consider analyzing character in a classroom context. What does this have to do with students' lives and futures? Well, if we can agree that we get one life to live, then literature is one of the few options we have to explore other lives. Smith and Wilhelm (2010) state this beautifully: Literature allows us to put on perspectives other than our own and to test what comes from adopting those perspectives. Literature lets us to try out new ways of being or acting- to rehearse what we might say or do in new situations. Throughout their lives our students will benefit from putting on new perspectives, and in teaching character analysis we are teaching them that the world is interpreted through a myriad of lenses. To navigate that world, it is helpful to recognize that our lens does not represent the only perspective, and that taking on the perspectives of others can lead us to better relationships and life experiences whether in resolving conflicts or working within a team. Analyzing character helps us practice for those future interactions while also exploring the primary question of psychology based careers – what makes people behave the way they do? The activities related to character in this resource have been successful in leading students towards deeper character analysis, but they also provide opportunity for students to grow into their futures by developing skills and exploring concepts that will serve them throughout life.

> Throughout their lives our students will benefit from putting on new perspectives, and in teaching character analysis we are teaching them that the world is interpreted through a myriad of lenses.

In exploring setting we can further see the relationship between classroom learning and the *real* world. Because setting is not just time and place, but also relationships that exist between characters and concentric circles of micro-social settings, and meso-social settings that together create a decision-making context in which characters operate (Smith & Wilhelm, 2010). In other words, the setting provides the psychology and the rules, and how the characters respond to those rules within that psychological environment tells the reader about the character. There are three expanding circles of setting: Micro, meso, and macro settings. Micro settings are the smallest circles followed by meso then macro. In *Romeo and Juliet,* an example of a micro-setting might be Friar Lawrence's cell, while a meso setting might be Verona as a whole, and a macro setting might be the world of teenagers in love. These concentric circles of setting are strikingly similar to the complexities of context that students must navigate in their lives now and into the future. For instance, a student athlete operates within the micro-social setting of her family in which she is motivated to be successful at sports because of the expectations placed on her by that social setting. Because she is a high school track star her father supports her athletic pursuits, her family values sportsmanship, so she works to excel in that area to gain approval. At a meso-social setting is the presence of the greater track organization and school life. Within this setting, the athlete's muscular frame is less valued, unless it is producing wins for the team. Being pretty and fashionable has greater importance, and so, in this setting, the female athlete is less valued for her athletic skill, and feels lack of success in this expanded social setting, so she makes different decisions. Perhaps when given an opportunity to try out for a higher-level team within the meso social setting she would decline, but if the invitation was presented within her micro-social setting she would jump at the chance! This is because different settings motivate characters in different ways. Within the activities in this resource, students will explore how setting affects behavior through deeply and closely reading the text as well as contemplating resetting their production entirely and investigating the effects on the characters.

## Instruction: Learning Goals

The learning goals for this chapter are related to describing the story elements of plot, setting and character, and explaining how these elements interact to create the whole story. At the beginning of the continuum students work to simply describe plot, character, and setting in detail. As students progress, the work becomes more complex as they look at how a character responds to challenges and reflects on a topic related to the theme of the story. At this stage students are also beginning to consider the relationship between a character's decisions and the plot.

Stating learning goals directly will help students identify the purpose of instruction and thus be more likely to achieve it. Specifically, the activities in this module will help students explore the ways in which character, setting and plot work together to create a story. This can be stated as follows for students: I can describe the plot, setting, and characters, and explain how they interact.

### Module Learning Goals

| | Going Far | | | | |
|---|---|---|---|---|---|
| | 4 | 5 | 6 | 7 | 8 |
| Character, setting, and plot. | Describe a character, setting or plot event in depth. | Compare and contrast two or more characters, settings, or plot events in detail. | Describe how characters respond or change as the plot moves forward. | Explain how different story elements interact and effect each other. | Explain how lines of dialogue or events drive the action forward, reveal character or force a decision to be made. |
| | Going Deep | | | | |
| | Plot: I created and labeled a plot diagram using tableau scenes. | | | | |
| | Plot: I completed a SCAMPER plot analysis. | | | | |
| | Setting: I researched Shakespeare's setting and presented my findings. | | | | |
| | Setting: I reflected on how the setting in which action occurs effects the choices that characters make. | | | | |
| | Character: I created a character's choices map to show how a character's choices affect the plot. | | | | |
| | Character: I wrote and/or performed in an unseen scene. | | | | |

The benchmarks for this learning goal were established using the Common Core Standards.

## Assessments

The following prompts increase in complexity and can be used as an assessment tool. Student responses may come in various product forms including a written or spoken response, a student designed and completed graphic organizer, or a digital presentation using the application of choice.

Choose a character, setting, and plot event to describe in detail. Use text evidence to support your description.

Choose two or more characters, settings, and plot events. Explain their similarities and differences. Use text evidence to support your thinking.

Choose a moment of the plot in which a major event or change happens. Describe how two different characters respond to the change or event and how their response moves the plot forward. Use text evidence to support your thinking.

Choose two different story elements. Explain how the two elements interact and affect each other. Use text evidence to support your thinking.

Choose a line of dialogue from the text or an important event. Then, explain how the dialogue or event moves the plot forward, reveals character, or forces a character to make a decision.

## Instruction Learning Activities: "I Can Determine Plot"

### Activity 1: Revisiting Tableaux and Comics

During the close read process described in Chapter 2, students may have created tableaux and comic strips. These items can be either created now or reused in the following activity to further solidify the plot of the stories should students need reinforcement. Tableaux are frozen scenes, photographed, and printed they become student featured playing cards in a plot organization game. Comic strips created to quickly record the plot via a beginning, middle and end panel for each act can be used similarly.

**Time:** One to two class periods.

**Materials:**

- Three-panel comic strip sheets.
- Camera.
- Giant paper to arrange plot diagrams.

**Steps:**

1. If students have not created them, have students create a three-panel strip for each act, or scene. Doing panels for each scene creates more panels to work with. Creating panels for each act forces students to think critically about what events are most important. Alternately, students can create and photograph a tableau for each act or scene.
2. Once the comics or tableaux are created print a set of tableaux photographs or copy a set of comics for each team or partnership of students. Neither tableaux nor photographs should be labeled with scenes or acts on the copies. Students can then use the sets to complete any of the following activities.
    a. **Construct a Plot Diagram** – After reviewing the components of plot, students create a plot diagram using the set of comics. Diagrams should be labeled with exposition, rising action, climax, falling action, and resolution.
    b. **Identify and Defend** – Students select and identify pivotal plot scenes from the tableaux. Using evidence from the text and details presented in the scene, they must make a claim about what scene is being depicted and support their claim.
    c. **Create a Comic From the Tableaux** – Students reconstruct the story using tableau photographs that were turned into comics with the addition of speech and thought bubbles.
    d. **Story Arcs within Story Arcs** – Students use individual comic panels or tableaux to reconstruct the story arcs within the stories to illustrate the complexities of Shakespeare's plots.

## Activity 2: Character's Choices Plot Map

An important concept for students to understand is the fact that character's decisions affect the plot. To explore this concept, students will create a map of the plot creating a Y in the path at each decision point and labeling accordingly. In doing so students will generate another visualization of the plot, as well as an alternate story. This activity also illustrates how stories must have characters in conflict in order to exist. For example, had Hermia not argued with her father and chosen to run off rather than obey him there would be no story, or at the very least it would be a short lived tale of a sad girl who accepted her fate.

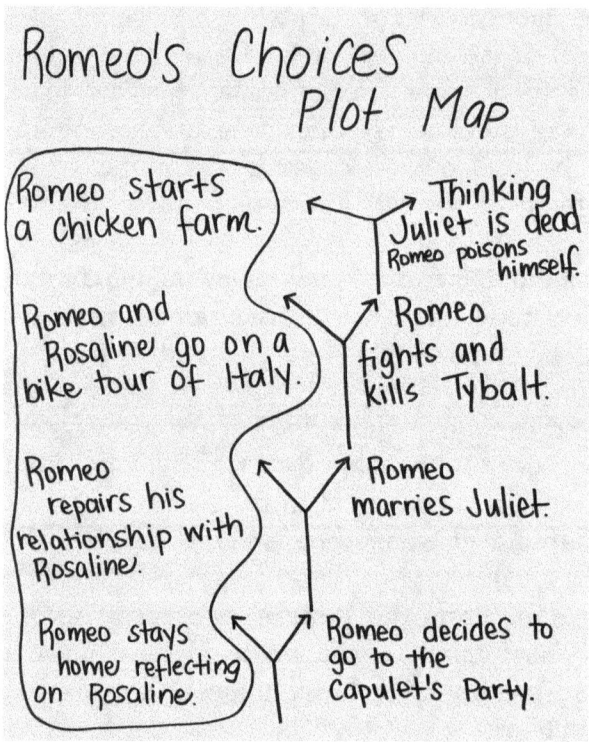

**FIGURE 3.1** A map of the choices made, and those not made, creates a visual representations of how a character's decisions shape the plot.

**Time:** This activity can be done quickly in one class session, or over several sessions if a text dependent writing or creative writing element is included.

**Materials:**

- Large chart paper.
- Markers.

**Steps:**

1. Students, either individually or in partnership, select a character to analyze. Characters can also be assigned. There will most likely be multiple teams working with the same character. This is perfectly fine and will allow for meaningful discussion at the conclusion. Avoid putting all students working on one character in the same group. This activity works better in smaller teams.
2. Instruct students to consider their character and what choices they made at the very beginning of the story. What was the character's first choice? Draw that choice as a Y on the paper. Label the lower portion of the Y with the choice itself. Label one fork of the Y with the decision they made. Label the other fork with a decision they could have made, but did not.
3. From the fork of the Y that indicates the choice made, have students construct a connecting path that turns into a second Y. This second Y represents the character's next decision. Repeat the labeling process: Label the lower portion of the Y with the choice itself. Label one fork of the Y with the decision they made. Label the other fork with a decision they could have made, but did not. Continue this process until students have recorded each decision point, or at least 4–6 major decisions throughout the story, on their map.
4. Students may illustrate their map with corresponding images or symbolism, or perhaps with character traits leading to the decisions made.
5. Once the maps depict the character's decision-making journey, then students should all be instructed to trace the path of decisions made on their maps. This illustrates the plot from one perspective: character's choices. The following questions allow for deeper exploration.
    a. How many other plot lines might exist had the character made different choices throughout the story? Describe one of those alternate plots.
    b. How do character's choices affect plot? How do plot and character work together to create a story?
    c. How much does a character's traits affect plot?

6. At this point students may either write a different version of the story based on their plot and character choice maps, or they might treat one of the above questions as a text dependent question and respond in writing.

### Activity 3: SCAMPER the Plot

SCAMPER, or substitute, combine, adapt, maximize or minimize, put to another use, eliminate and reverse, is a creative thinking strategy used in business and design to generate ideas for new products and services. It has been shown to be an effective classroom strategy for developing creative thinking (Özyaprak, 2016). It can be employed by students to consider how the plot would be affected if certain changes were made, which in turn can give them the courage and spark needed to make their Shakespearean production their own. SCAMPER drives new possibilities into reality because it forces students to think in unconventional ways. Each letter stands for a different directive that is applied. In working through each directive new possibilities emerge. The SCAMPER strategy is based on the idea that what is new is actually a modification of existing old things. Film makers and stage directors have been reimagining Shakespeare for hundreds of years. Why shouldn't students be granted the same creative freedom? This exercise will help get them to a place where they are imagining the possibilities of staging Shakespeare through their own lenses.

**Time:** One to two class periods.
**Materials:**

- Critical Thinking: SCAMPER Chart.

## Critical Thinking: SCAMPER the Plot

Scholar's Name: _____

Question for Consideration: _____

_____

| Try… | My Thinking |
|---|---|
| **SUBSTITUTE** <br> Discuss the first letter, S. In SCAMPER, S tells us to substitute. Substituting requires us to think about these questions: What can we replace with something else? <br><br> **Thinking help:** <br> What if *Romeo and Juliet* was set in the deserts of Mexico? If we replaced Verona with Sonoran Desert what might Friar Lawrence be called? What medicines might he have concocted from the flora and fauna of the desert to help Juliet? | |
| **COMBINE** <br> Discuss the second letter, C. In SCAMPER, C tells us to combine. Combining requires us to think about these questions: What might we put together or combine? An example might be animation. Could we combine animation with live action for our performance? <br><br> **Thinking help:** <br> Could we combine gaming and this old-fashioned story? <br> What would happen if we combined Pokémon and *A Midsummer Night's Dream*? How would the story be the same? Be different? | |

Copyright material from Jennifer Szwaya (2024), *Shakespeare Amazes in the Classroom*, Routledge

| Try… | My Thinking  |
|---|---|
| **ADAPT**<br>Discuss the third letter, A. In SCAMPER, A tells us to adapt. Adapting requires us to think about these questions: What might we use in a new way?<br>Thinking helpers:<br>What if the magic flower in *A Midsummer Night's Dream*, or Friar's potion in *Romeo and Juliet*, or the poison put on the sword in *Hamlet* had not worked as expected? What if we adapted those items to function differently? How would the plot change? | |
| **MAXIMIZE or MINIMIZE**<br>Discuss the fourth letter, M. In SCAMPER, M tells us to minimize or maximize. Minimizing or Maximizing requires us to think about these questions: What might we increase or decrease?<br><br>**Thinking Help:**<br>What if in *Romeo and Juliet* we increased the amount of times Rosaline appeared in the story? Or decreased Tybalt's sense of honor? What if we increased the number of times the ghost appeared in *Hamlet*? What if we decreased the power fathers have over their daughters in *A Midsummer Night's Dream*? | |

Copyright material from Jennifer Szwaya (2024), *Shakespeare Amazes in the Classroom*, Routledge

Elements of the Story ◆ 63

| Try... | My Thinking |
|---|---|
| **PUT TO ANOTHER USE**<br>Discuss the fifth letter, P. In SCAMPER, P tells us to put to another use. Putting to another use requires us to think about these questions: What is something that is used for one thing that could be used for another?<br><br>**Thinking Help:**<br>What if the magic flower in *A Midsummer Night's Dream* had another function? What if Hamlet had seen something other than a ghost appear as his father? | |
| **ELIMINATE**<br>Discuss the sixth letter, E. In SCAMPER, E tells us to eliminate. Eliminating requires us to think about these questions: What might we get rid of?<br><br>**Thinking Help:**<br>Could we get rid of the sad ending in *Romeo and Juliet*? *Hamlet*? What would happen to the story? | |
| **REVERSE**<br>Discuss the seventh letter, R. In SCAMPER, R tells us to reverse. Reversing requires us to think about these questions: Could the characters literally reverse their course of action?<br><br>**Thinking Help:**<br>If they had the power to reverse their actions, what would they have learned? How would they redo their lives if they could reverse? What point might they reverse back to? | |

Copyright material from Jennifer Szwaya (2024), *Shakespeare Amazes in the Classroom*, Routledge

**Steps:**

1. Explain to students that they are going to use a creative thinking tool called SCAMPER to reimagine Shakespeare's work.
2. Discuss the first letter, S. In SCAMPER, S tells us to substitute. Substituting requires us to think about these questions:
   a. What can we replace with something else?
   b. What if *Romeo and Juliet* was set in the deserts of Mexico? If we replaced Verona with Sonoran Desert what might Friar Lawrence be called? What medicines might he have concocted from the flora and fauna of the desert to help Juliet?
3. Discuss the second letter, C. In SCAMPER, C tells us to combine. Combining requires us to think about these questions:
   a. What might we put together or combine? An example might be animation. Could we combine animation with live action for our performance?
   b. Could we combine gaming and this old-fashioned story?
   c. What would happen if we combined Pokémon and *A Midsummer Night's Dream*? How would the story be the same? Be different?
4. Discuss the third letter, A. In SCAMPER, A tells us to adapt. Adapting requires us to think about these questions:
   a. What might we use in a new way?
   b. What if the magic flower in *A Midsummer Night's Dream*, or the Friar's potion in *Romeo and Juliet*, or the poison put on the sword in *Hamlet* had not worked as expected? What if we adapted those items to function differently? How would the plot change?
5. Discuss the fourth letter, M. In SCAMPER, M tells us to minimize or maximize. Minimizing or maximizing requires us to think about these questions:
   a. What might we increase or decrease?
   b. What if in *Romeo and Juliet* we increased the amount of times Rosaline appeared in the story? Or decreased Tybalt's sense of honor?

c. What if we increased the number of times the ghost appeared in *Hamlet*?
   d. What if we decreased the power fathers have over their daughters in *A Midsummer Night's Dream*?
6. Discuss the fifth letter, P. In SCAMPER, P tells us to put to another use. Putting to another use requires us to think about these questions:
   a. What is something that is used for one thing that could be used for another?
   b. What if the magic flower in *A Midsummer Night's Dream* had another function? What if Hamlet had seen something other than a ghost appear as his father?
7. Discuss the sixth letter, E. In SCAMPER, E tells us to eliminate. Eliminating requires us to think about these questions:
   a. What might we get rid of?
   b. Could we get rid of the sad ending in *Romeo and Juliet*? *Hamlet*? What would happen to the story?
8. Discuss the seventh letter, R. In SCAMPER, R tells us to reverse. Reversing requires us to think about these questions:
   a. Could the characters literally reverse their course of action? If they had the power to reverse their actions what would they have learned? How would they redo their lives if they could reverse? What point might they reverse back to?
9. As students work through these thinking exercises, sharing the following questions can support the conversation:
   a. Is this change something that would be consistent with the way these characters behave?
   b. How might that change affect the theme?
   c. What new conflicts might arise? What conflicts might disappear?
   d. If we made that change would there still be a story?
   e. Which changes do you think would be important to include if we want to create a production that speaks to the lives of people your age?

## Learning Activities: "I Can Determine Setting"

**FIGURE 3.2** Dress rehearsal occurs within a highly detailed, student created setting.

Note: In this chapter, an engraving of Shakespeare's face by Charles Droeshout (1623) has been used to protect children's identities in photographs.

### Activity 1: Playing with Setting

The setting in which action occurs affects the choices that characters make. For instance, in Act 3 Scene 3, Hamlet finds Claudius praying alone. It is the perfect time to avenge his father's murder, but he decides not to precisely because of the setting in which he finds Claudius. Would the tale end differently if Hamlet had found Claudius in the stables? Or in a restaurant in a different time period? In contemplating this question: How would the characters behave differently in a different setting? Students develop a more complex and more accurate understanding of setting as not only a place and a time, but a place and a time that also effect behavior.

**Time:** At least one class session.
**Materials:**

- A deck of setting cards. These can be created by giving each student an index card and having them write down a setting.

Older students can add detail related to the micro and macro elements of the selected setting if appropriate to class learning goals. Examples of settings that might be featured on cards are the local high school or middle school, Starbucks, a restaurant, and another country such as Mexico or Poland.

**Steps:**

1. Review with students the basic definition of setting as time and place. Discuss an example of how they may behave differently in different settings even in the same circumstance. For instance, not being prepared for class may be handled differently in different classrooms. In one classroom in which the teacher is understanding and lenient, an unprepared student may be direct with the teacher about not being prepared for class, however in another room where more strict rules prevail, the student might lie in order to avoid being embarrassed. Same situation, different settings, different choices made.
2. Explain that we will be considering different characters' choices in different settings.
3. Choose a situation from the ones provided and discuss how they responded as well as how the setting may have affected their response.
4. After organizing students into cooperative learning groups, have each group select a setting card. The group should consider how the character would respond should the setting be changed to the one on the card.
5. Finally, teams share their thinking and discuss.

## Examples: Characters' Choices

### *A Midsummer Night's Dream*
The setting of *A Midsummer Night's Dream* is during a time when women had little agency over their own decisions. Rather, their lives were decided by fathers and husbands. We know this because of Egeus' lines which the duke agrees with: "I beg the ancient privilege of Athens, as she is mine, I may dispose of her:

Which shall be either to this gentleman or to her death according to our law." Egeus decides that he would rather have his daughter put to death for disobeying him, than to have her choose who she loves and marries. If Egeus had to make this decision in another time or place, would he?

The theme of female agency is continued in Act 2 Scene 2 where Oberon puts the love potion on Titania's eyes. He is mad at her for not giving him what he wants, so he seeks revenge through the potion which will make her fall in love with the first thing she sees upon waking. Puck has the mission of finding a vile creature for her to fall in love with. One must wonder whether if the circumstances of the setting were different, would Oberon act in such a vengeful manner? For instance, what if these were not fairies in Athens? Would Oberon's feelings about how to treat women be different? What if the conflict between Oberon and Titania had been about something else, or what if Titania had compromised with Oberon and let him work with the boy from time to time? Would Oberon have made the same decision if the circumstances of the setting were different?

## *Romeo and Juliet*

Act 1 Scene 1 is filled with characters making choices. Sampson, who is presumably hanging out with Gregory in the middle of a public place in Verona, initially seems to want to remain reserved rather than instigate a fight with the Montagues whom they see coming into the same public space. When egged on to draw his sword by Gregory, Sampson replies that he'd rather "let them begin." But, when Gregory confirms that he is going to instigate, then Sampson makes the decision to "bite my thumb at him." This is a very rude gesture to make, and it escalates the conflict which ultimately results in a street fight that has to be disbanded by the Prince himself. What if, however, the setting had not been a public place where Sampson and Gregory were hanging out? What if they had been elsewhere? Would Gregory have found it necessary to instigate the situation in a different setting?

Later, the conflict becomes further escalated by Tybalt, who is given a choice by Benvolio to assist him in separating the

Montagues and Capulets to keep the peace, or to continue escalating the situation. Tybalt chooses to escalate in this setting, but an interesting question to ask is in what setting might Tybalt have taken Benvolio up on his idea to work together?

At the end of Act 1, Scene 4, Romeo chooses to enter the Capulets' party despite having fears of "consequence yet hanging in the stars." If he was in a situation in which he was fearful of the consequences, would he still go forward if his friends were not present?

In Act 1 Scene 5, Lord Capulet, when informed by Tybalt that enemy Montagues are present at the party, commands Tybalt to leave them alone rather than allow a fight to occur. Would he have made that same choice if the setting was not a festive party? In what setting would Lord Capulet allow an altercation to occur?

Act 3 Scene 1 is the one in which the young members of the Montagues and Capulets fight again as Tybalt seeks to restore the honor stolen by Romeo and his friends when they attended the Capulets' party. These young men each make decisions in this scene which lead to death and banishment. This scene begs the following questions be considered and debated: Do kids act differently in the company of certain friends? How do rules and expectations vary from peer group to peer group, and how do those expectations affect decisions made in those different settings? To what degree are decisions affected by the rules of these two peer groups? Would the outcome of this scene be different if the setting was different? How would it need to change to affect a different outcome?

In Act 4 Scene 1, Juliet and Friar Lawrence make decisions that one could argue are affected by the setting. In this scene Juliet asks for the Friar's help in escaping her father's command to marry Paris. This situation is set in a time in which, as we know, the Montagues and Capulets are feuding, and Juliet is in extreme distress over having to marry Paris when she is already married and in love with Romeo. Under such circumstances, the Friar made the decision to help Juliet thinking that perhaps a marriage between the houses would end the feud. And Juliet made the decision to execute the Friar's plan. Had the Montagues and Capulets not been fighting, perhaps the Friar would not have helped Juliet because he would not have the same rationale as there would be no feud to end. Juliet, if in a calmer frame of mind, may not have gone along with the Friar's plan. The time in which these decisions took place affected the choice being made. How might Juliet and the Friar's choices have been different if the setting was different?

### *Hamlet*

In Act 1 Scene 2, Horatio, who is a guard of Elsinore, makes the decision to share with Hamlet that he, Marcellus, and Bernardo saw the ghost of King Hamlet. Consider the setting in which Horatio and Hamlet know each other. How would their relationship be different if they were just two friends playing video games rather than prince and guard? Or what if Hamlet saw Horatio's father as a ghost?

Later, in the same scene, Hamlet decides not to return to Wittenburg. What about the setting might have driven him to that decision? What decision might he make if the setting were different? How would the setting have to change?

In Act 1 Scene 4, Hamlet makes the decision to stand guard with Horatio and Marcellus so that he might get a chance to see the ghost of his father. Later, Hamlet makes the decision to follow the ghost when he does appear. Would he make the same decision if the setting were not guarding his own castle with his guard friends? What if guards loyal to Claudius were out that night? What if Ophelia had seen the ghost and the setting involved her and no friendly guards?

In Act 2 Scene 2, Polonius makes the decision to tell Claudius about the conflict between Hamlet and Ophelia. If this were set elsewhere would he have kept her confidence? What is it about the setting of Elsinore Castle that might have led Polonius to make that choice?

In Act 3 Scene 3, Hamlet finds Claudius confessing to murder in the chapel. Hamlet struggles with deciding whether or not to kill him, but he ultimately decides not to. Why? What role does the setting have in this decision?

## Activity 2: Reimagining the Story in a Different Setting

Shakespeare's plays have been reinterpreted countless times. Most modern and innovative performances update the setting. Because place evokes identity, giving students agency over the setting allows students to make the production their own. This is a very powerful experience for students. This activity should be completed early in the process of planning the performance so that students have time to consider whether or not they want to reset the story in another time or place.

**Time:** One or more class sessions.
**Materials:**

- Reimagined Setting Think Sheet.
- Clips and examples of different stagings and interpretations of either *Hamlet*, *Romeo and Juliet*, or *A Midsummer Night's Dream* depending on the class's focus.

**Steps:**

1. Discuss with students the various interpretations of Shakespeare that have been staged over time.
2. Review the conflicts and characters central to the drama being studied. Then ask students where they might find similar conflicts, or how those conflicts and characters might be different if set elsewhere. See the multimedia chapter and the list within this lesson, for film clips that demonstrate the fact that film makers and creators have been reimagining Shakespeare's work for centuries.
3. Brainstorm and discuss a possible list of settings that are relevant to students lives. Examples might be cities or countries related to student's culture and heritage, a present-day school, the neighborhood in which students live etc.
4. Divide the class into teams or partnerships and have each select a setting from the brainstormed list as the basis for completing the Reimagining Setting Sheet.
5. After completing the think sheets, student groups should share out their findings.

6. Finally, students can vote to determine where they will set their production. Materials from this activity can then be used to inform the scenery/props teams and the script writing teams about how they will proceed.

## A Midsummer Night's Dream

- *A Midsummer Night's Cirque* is a retelling in a Cirque du Soleil atmosphere performed by Theater Arts Lab Series at Dominican University in Illinois.
- A silent film version was created in 1925 called *Wood Love* by Hans Newman.
- *A Midsummer Night's Dream* has also been set in modern-day Los Angeles and in a futuristic world by independent film companies in the United States and the United Kingdom.
- Disney created an animated short of *A Midsummer Night's Dream* starring Mickey as Lysander, Minnie as Hermia, Daisy Duck as Helena, and Donald Duck as Demetrius.

## Romeo and Juliet

- *Gnomeo and Juliet* is an animated retelling set in a present-day garden.
- *West Side Story* is a revision set in New York City.
- *The Sea Prince and the Fire Child* is a 1981 Japanese anime film by Sanrio Is a retelling of star-crossed lovers that mirrors *Romeo and Juliet*, which is in itself, like *Cinderella*, a story that appears across a variety of different cultures. The setting is entirely fantastical.
- *Romeo y Julieta*, created in 1943, is a farcical retelling from Mexico.
- *Mônica e Cebolinha: No Mundo de Romeu e Julieta*, created in 1978, is an animated version of the play from Brazil.
- There is a German version set at a summer camp, versions from India and Egypt, a version that features rival football clubs, and even a version told through ice skating!

## Hamlet

- The television show *Sons of Anarchy* is a retelling of Hamlet, set in present-day California, in which kings are replaced with motorcycle gangs.
- Disney's *The Lion King* is a retelling of *Hamlet* set in the African savannah.
- *The Angel of Vengeance* is a 1977 Turkish remake of *Hamlet* in which the lead character is female.

### Activity 3: Visiting Shakespeare's Settings

The anchor texts for this book, *Hamlet, Romeo and Juliet,* and *A Midsummer Night's Dream,* are all set in places that can be visited today. This provides an excellent opportunity to develop a concrete sense of place through photographs. Developing schema with images prior to reading is also an excellent way to reach multilingual learners.

**Time:** Three to four class sessions.

**Materials:**

- Technology that allows students to share images with classmates. A simple slide show application will work well. Students will also need access to google or another search engine that will allow students to access images.
- Reimagining Setting Sheet.

**Steps:**

1. After organizing students into partnerships, explain that the partnerships are on a mission to find photographs that represent the place in which the story they are studying takes place. Alternately, images can be selected and printed ahead of time by the teacher. Images can be placed in envelopes for student teams to select at random.
2. Assign topics to teams, or allow teams to select topics for themselves.

3. Students create a slide show of 3–5 images. For each photograph, students record notes to answer the following reflective questions:
   a. What do you notice in the pictures?
   b. What details tell us about the time period? Consider the architecture, clothing, and objects.
   c. Who lives in this place? Describe the people that might live here.
   d. What is the mood of this place?
   e. What kind of activities might happen here?
   f. What type of rules or expectations might exist in this setting?
4. Students can take turns sharing their findings with the larger group or by joining another partnership to discuss. This can also be done as a gallery walk in which students play their slideshows on individual devices that the class rotates among.
5. Finally, after collecting information about each photograph students complete a quick write to describe the settings portrayed in one of the images, or they write a story set in three different images within a team.

## A Midsummer Night's Dream

- Athens, Greece in a forest.
- Briars and brambles.

## Romeo and Juliet

- Verona, Italy.
- Mantua, Italy.

## Hamlet

- Denmark.
- Elsinore Castle – located in the town of Helsingør, Denmark (the English translation of Helsingør is Elsinore), Kronborg castle is Shakespeare's Elsinore.
- Court.

# Learning Activities: "I Can Determine Character"

## Activity 1: First Impressions and Checkpoints

This can be done in conjunction with the close read routine described in Chapter 3. It was inspired by the work of Smith and Wilhelm (2010) who described the process of getting to know a character in a text as a series of checkpoints in which the reader collects new information about a character as they read, and then compares new knowledge to what is known about the character in order to determine whether or not the character has changed. There is an online editable resource titled Critical Thinking: First Impressions and Check Ins available for this activity.

This activity is done while reading and prepares students for the ubiquitous type of assessment questions that ask them to explain how a character changed over time. After first meeting a character in Act 1, students record their initial impressions of that character. Then, students continue reading, pausing to record information about the character in each act. Students analyze the character through multiple lenses of their words, thoughts, actions, memberships, appearance, and choices. After reading and collecting notes and/or direct quotations from the text, students reflect on whether or not their impression of the character changed, and/or if the character themselves changed. Students should be encouraged to analyze the character of their choice. This activity can be done individually or in groups. A debriefing conversation at the conclusion of each session would maximize learning for all students.

This activity can be enhanced by using the film clips outlined in the multimedia chapter as a secondary text.

**Time:** Six 15–20-minute sessions; This could be an excellent center type activity.

**Materials:**

- Critical Thinking: First Impressions and Check Ins

## Critical Thinking: Checking In with Characters

Scholar's Name _____

Purpose of Reading: The purpose of this reading is to consider a character of your choice. As you read, reflect on the character you selected, and whether or not your first impression of them changes. Finally consider whether the character themselves changed, and in what ways.

| Act 1: After reading Act 1, record your first impressions of _____ _____. What kind of person is _____? |||
|---|---|---|
| **Act 2: Checkpoint:** Add any notes or quotes under the correct category as you read Act 2. |||
| Groups/Teams/Partnerships | Thoughts | Actions |
| Choices | Appearance | Words |
| **Act 3: Checkpoint:** Add any notes or quotes under the correct category as you read Act 3. |||
| Groups/Teams/Partnerships | Thoughts | Actions |
| Choices | Appearance | Words |

Copyright material from Jennifer Szwaya (2024), *Shakespeare Amazes in the Classroom*, Routledge

Elements of the Story ♦ 77

| Act 4: Checkpoint: Add any notes or quotes under the correct category as you read Act 4. | | |
|---|---|---|
| Groups/Teams/ Partnerships | Thoughts | Actions |
| Choices | Appearance | Words |

| Act 5: Checkpoint: Add any notes or quotes under the correct category as you read Act 5. | | |
|---|---|---|
| Groups/Teams/ Partnerships | Thoughts | Actions |
| Choices | Appearance | Words |

Concluding Reflection:
In what ways did your first impression of the character change?

In what ways did the character themselves change?

Copyright material from Jennifer Szwaya (2024), *Shakespeare Amazes in the Classroom*, Routledge

**Steps:**

1. Students determine which character they would like to analyze. This is a great opportunity to get to know the character they will be performing, so if parts have been claimed by the time this activity is assigned, then students might be encouraged to work with the character they will be playing. Students might be partnered up or placed in small groups at this point. Explain the different ways good readers think about characters by reminding students that good readers often consider a character's words, thoughts, actions, choices, appearance, and relationships when determining who a character is as they read.
2. Students read Act 1 reflecting on their chosen character. After, they do a quick write to record their initial impression of the character. Who is this character as a human being? Before moving on students should be given an opportunity to share their thinking with students who are analyzing *different* characters.
3. Students continue reading Act 2. As they read, students record either notes or direct quotes under the corresponding category individually of within their small groups. Before moving on students working on analyzing the *same* character should be given an opportunity to share their thinking. These steps should be repeated for Acts 3–5.
4. Finally, students analyze their findings within their same character teams and record their thinking.
5. This activity can easily be extended to include a compare and contrast element. Students can partner with a peer who analyzed a different character and together construct a written response to show similarities and differences.

## Activity 2: Unseen Scenes

Throughout *Hamlet*, *Romeo and Juliet*, and *Midsummer*, there are scenes which the reader knows must have happened, but do not actually take place. Write diary entries, or create monologues to add to the play that show multiple perspectives on how that conversation may have gone. Students choose the character from whose perspective they should write, and then the assessment comes from the defense of their choices and how evidence for that character's characterization demonstrates their ability to understand who a character is. The following bullets provide points in the story in which a scene is not shown, but is known to have taken place.

## A Midsummer Night's Dream

- Conversation between Hermia's parents before Egeus visits Theseus the duke.
- Conversation in which Helena tells Demetrius about Hermia and Lysander running off.

## Romeo and Juliet

- By the end of Act 1 Scene 2, we know that Romeo is depressed because a girl named Rosaline is not returning his love. We the reader never meet Rosaline, but we know they must have interacted.
- The conversation between Juliet and her nurse as she was getting ready for the Capulets' party might be interesting to consider. We know Romeo's motivational mindset as he entered the party, but what was Juliet thinking?

## Hamlet

- Conversation between Gertrude and Claudius prior to King Hamlet's murder.
- First meeting between Hamlet and Ophelia.

**Activity 3: Cure for a Conflict**

This character representation activity requires students to think critically, evaluate, and summarize as they describe characters while also creatively connecting to the botany and early chemistry woven throughout Shakespeare. From the poisons used by murderers in *Hamlet*, to the potions distributed by Friar Lawrence in *Romeo and Juliet* to the magical flowers in *A Midsummer Night's Dream*, plants are constantly playing starring roles in Shakespeare's stories. In this activity, students consider a problem that a character faces and what character traits worked to create the problem. Looking at a chart of medicinal botanicals used during Shakespeare's time, students create a representation of the potion that would solve the character's problem. After creating their medicines, a debrief and sharing activity would allow for excellent discussion opportunities as students agree, disagree, and defend their thinking with text evidence.

**Time:** Two class sessions.
**Materials:**

- Critical Thinking: Shakespeare's Botanicals

# Critical Thinking: Shakespeare's Botanicals

Scholar's Name: _____

## Botanical Supplies

| Botanical | Property | Shakespeare's Reference |
|---|---|---|
| Rosemary | • Reduces stress.<br>• Improves memory and concentration.<br>• Improves eye health and vision problems. | Ophelia: "There's Rosemary, That's for remembrance; Remember, pray, love."<br>*Hamlet*, Act 4, Scene 5.<br><br>Friar Lawrence: "Dry up your tears and put Rosemary on this fair course."<br>*Romeo and Juliet*, Act 4 Scene 5. |
| Fennel<br>Columbine | • Improves digestion issues and loss of appetite.<br>• Visual problems.<br>• Treats headaches, fevers.<br>• Works as a love charm. | Ophelia: "There's Fennel for you and Columbines."<br>*Hamlet*, Act 4 Scene 5. |
| Cowslip | • Improves insomnia.<br>• Treats hysteria.<br>• Treats weak hearts.<br>• Treats nervousness. | Faeries: "The cowslips tall her pensioners be; In their gold coats spots you see; Those be rubies, fairy favours; In those freckles live their savours; I must go seek some dewdrops here, And hang a pearl in every cowslip's ear."<br>*A Midsummer Night's Dream*, Act 2, Scene 1 |
| Crow flowers<br><br>Nettles<br><br>Daisies | • Treats wounds and infections.<br><br>• Reduces blood sugar to improve thinking.<br><br>• Improves vision and treats pain. | Gertrude: "There with fantastic garlands did she come Of crow flowers, nettles, daisies, And long purples."<br>*Hamlet*, Act 4 Scene 7 |

Copyright material from Jennifer Szwaya (2024), *Shakespeare Amazes in the Classroom*, Routledge

| Garlic | • Helps calm and control blood pressure. | Bottom: "Most dear actors eat no onions or Garlicke For we are to utter sweet breath." *A Midsummer Night's Dream*, Act 2 Scene 1 |
|---|---|---|
| Hazelnuts | • Improves brain health<br>• Improves memory. | Mercutio: "Her chariot is a hazelnut" *Romeo and Juliet*, Act 2 Scene 4 |

Description of the character including their problem:

_____
_____
_____
_____

Suggested Potion and Recipe

_____
_____

Potion Recipe                    Potion Illustration




Copyright material from Jennifer Szwaya (2024), *Shakespeare Amazes in the Classroom*, Routledge

Explanation of why this mixture, more than any other, will help the character manage the problem described.

_____
_____
_____
_____
_____
_____
_____
_____
_____
_____

Explanation of how this mixture will improve the character's life.

_____
_____
_____
_____
_____
_____
_____
_____
_____
_____

**Steps:**

1. Brainstorm a list of characters and their various problems with students so that they have a menu of characters and problems from which to choose. Welcome all reasonable student ideas.
2. Students select a character and one of their selected character's problems to analyze.
3. Next, students reflect on the character traits that that character has and how those traits might be making the problem more difficult for the character. Students consider what traits might be more helpful.
4. Using the resource Critical Thinking: Shakespeare's Botanicals students create a potion that will give the character the traits they need to solve their own problem.
5. Students present their potions and defend their thinking using text evidence.

## Considerations

Over the course of my career I have worked with several students who are twice exceptional. These students have high abilities and intelligence, and also have learning or behavior issues to manage. It has been my experience that students who are twice exceptional often have intense interests that occupy their thoughts nearly all of the time. It can be a challenge to persuade students with such strong interests to take a break with the Bard, so instead of trying to get the interest to take a nap while we study Shakespeare, I invite the child to consider their interest in conjunction with Shakespeare's characters. For instance, my friend Anthony was obsessed with Pokemon when he was in my class. Rather than engage in a power struggle, I worked to make his interest a part of his thinking by asking questions such as: Have any of their characters been in a similar situation to Hamlet? How is their situation the same and different? How would this character handle the decision that Hamlet had to make? How is the character's setting the same or different from Elsinore? Including student interests can be easier and more productive than engaging in a power struggle.

## Revisiting Essential Unit Question

In this module students work to examine character, plot, and setting because in determining the story elements of a text helps us comprehend or make sense of it. Therefore, we can say that language gives us systems like story elements to help us make sense of the world. Looking closer at each element's relationship to the real world, that is, the world outside of a student's classroom, reveals further information about the power of language. In examining character, we use language to learn about how people of the world and throughout time might behave, and some use language to help people who are making poor choices to make better choices. Examining setting also helps us develop a sense of the world in which we live as it has been throughout time and in different situations. Applying an understanding of setting as a time and place with specific rules that steer people's choices also gives it an avenue for understanding the people that take up space around us. Language gives us a way to apply those insights and to communicate about them together.

## Resources

This guide provides further detailed information about using tableaux within the classroom.

*Tableau*. (2023, May 17). https://waltonartscenter.org/global assets/wac/forms/smart_residency_tableau_study_guide_14.pdf.

## References

Lamb, C., & Lamb, M. (1807). *Tales from Shakespeare*. Juvenile Library of William Godwin.

McKnight, K. S. (2008). *The second city guide to improv in the classroom: Using improvisation to teach skills and boost learning*. Jossey-Bass.

National Governors Association Center for Best Practices & Council of Chief State School Officers. (2010). *Common core state standards for English language arts and literacy in history/social studies, science, and technical subjects*. Authors.

Özyaprak, M. (2016). The effectiveness of SCAMPER technique on creative thinking skills. *Journal for the Education of Gifted Young Scientists*, 4, 31–31. http://dx.doi.org/10.17478/JEGYS.2016116348.

Quealy, G., Hasegawa-Collins, S., & Mirren, H. (2018). *Botanical Shakespeare: An illustrated compendium of all the flowers, fruits, herbs, trees, seeds, and grasses cited by the world's greatest playwright*. Harper Design.

Shakespeare, W. (1596). *A midsummer night's dream*.

Shakespeare, W. (1597). *Romeo and Juliet*.

Shakespeare, W. (1601). *Hamlet*.

Smith, M. W., & Wilhelm, J. D. (2010). *Fresh takes on teaching literary elements: How to teach what really matters about character, setting, point of view and Theme*. Scholastic.

# 4

# Theme

In coaching teachers over the years I have, from time to time, seen theme taught in a limited way. That is to say, literary theme is taught as party theme. When throwing a birthday party, one might say that the theme is dinosaurs or princesses. One word generally explains what type of decorations and dress is appropriate. A literary theme cannot be stated as one word. Rather, one way to think of literary theme is as a word plus a "so what about it?" In other words, to describe the theme of *Romeo and Juliet* a student might say "it is a story about love." To which I would reply, "yes, I agree, but what about love? What is Shakespeare saying about love in *Romeo and Juliet*? What is he trying to teach us through their story?" The activities dealing with theme in this resource drive students to consider the message of the story at a more complex level of understanding, so that they can formulate the "so what" of theme, and find the evidence to support their thinking.

Real world connections to classroom learning should be made explicit, and theme can be related to real life as well. How does studying theme help current and future versions of students beyond the classroom? Theme is about recognizing life's patterns and lessons. Determining theme may be our most important work as readers because it makes us philosophers who are trying to determine the meaning of life. Stories are a slice of a life that we can examine under a microscope. We readers are

> In this way reading for theme is doing the most important work of our time on this planet – figuring out what the point of being here is.

like scientists examining that slice for the meaning of life. In this way, reading for theme is doing the most important work of our time on this planet – figuring out what the point of being here is.

## Instruction: Learning Goals

The learning goals for this chapter are related to determining the theme. At the beginning of the continuum students work to simply identify the theme, and as students progress, the work becomes more complex as they look at how theme develops across a text and how a character might reflect on a topic related to the theme of the story. At this stage students are also beginning to consider the relationship between a character's decisions and the theme. Finally students strive to understand how the author conveys the theme throughout the text.

Stating learning goals directly will help students identify the purpose of instruction and thus be more likely to achieve it. Specifically, the activities in this module will help students determine the theme of a text and explore the ways in which character, setting, and plot work together to communicate the theme. This can be stated as follows for students: I can determine the theme and explain how it is developed over the course of a text; I can describe the plot, setting, and characters, and explain how they relate to the theme.

### Module Learning Goals

| | Going Far | | | | |
|---|---|---|---|---|---|
| | 4 | 5 | 6 | 7 | 8 |
| Theme | Determine the theme. | Determine the theme including how characters respond to challenges. | Determine the theme including how characters reflect on a topic. | Determine the theme and analyze its development over the course of the text. | Determine the theme and analyze its development over the course of the text including its relationship to characters, setting and plot. |
| | **Going Deep** | | | | |
| | I completed an object reflection presentation. | | | | |
| | I wrote a letter of advice to a character. | | | | |
| | I reflected on the connection between theme and philosophy. | | | | |

The benchmarks for this learning goal were established using the Common Core Standards.

## Instruction: Assessments

The following prompts increase in complexity and can be used as an assessment tool. Student responses may come in various product forms including a written or spoken response, a student designed and completed graphic organizer, or a digital presentation using the application of choice.

What do you think is the theme of the text? Use evidence and examples from the text to support your thinking.

Consider how characters respond to challenges within the text. What is Shakespeare trying to teach the reader about life through those character's responses? Use text evidence to explain how character's choices reveal the theme.

Consider how characters reflect and ponder topics within the text. What is Shakespeare trying to teach the reader about life through those character's reflections? Use text evidence to explain how character's reflections reveal the theme.

Determine the theme of the text. Use evidence to explain how the theme is developed over the course of the text.

Determine the theme of the text. Use evidence to explain how the theme is developed over the course of the text through the characters, plot, and setting.

## Activities: "I Can Determine Theme"

Ultimately, when working with theme, I want students to be able to explain what the theme of the story is and how they know. The examples that follow illuminate where students' thinking might hover as they prepare a written response centered on theme. Activity 1 helps students think abstractly about theme and can be an inventive springboard into the introduction of their essay. Activities 2 and 3 prepare students to collect evidence as they reflect on possible themes.

Please note, student essays should not be limited to evidence highlighted in the following paragraphs about theme. Evidence highlighted is for the benefit of your preparation efforts and not meant as information that should be given to students, rather provided as an example in cases where an example is needed for the students to continue to make progress. Rely on the supplemental materials, the Lamb texts, and the Shortened Shakespeare texts to find supporting evidence. The text has been edited down so that students can focus on key scenes and dialogue in which to find their evidence. Most frequently discussed themes and scenes in which evidence might be selected to draw conclusions about what Shakespeare is teaching about a particular theme are outlined.

## *Hamlet*

In my experience, there are four themes within *Hamlet* that most often arise in students' questions during the first close reading of the Mary and Charles Lamb stories and sustain student interest through close readings of the original text. They are parenting, revenge, honesty, and friendship. Since students are taught that theme is not just a singular idea, but what the author might be trying to tell us about the human experience of that idea, as a class we interrogate that idea until we get a clear question, and eventually response from the author through the text. Such a conversation may sound like this.

> *Teacher: (Referring to the questions posted on posters from the first close reading)* After reading your questions for the text I noticed many of you were interested in the idea of friendship. Here are some of your example questions that led me to that conclusion: Are Rosencrantz and Guildenstern helping Hamlet? Why don't Marcellus and Horatio want Hamlet to follow the ghost? Why is Hamlet so unkind to Ophelia? Who is Hamlet's best friend?
> 
> *Student 1:* There are lots of bad relationships.
> *Student 2:* Not ALL bad.
> *Teacher:* Okay, any examples?
> *Student 2:* Horatio.
> *Teacher:* What about Horatio?
> *Student 2:* Well, he's sorta like Hamlet's spy during the play.
> *Teacher:* Ahh! Okay, I see a good friend must also be a spy.

*Students: (Roll eyes at the oversimplification.)*
*Teacher:* Who of these people would you want to be your friend?
*Student 1:* Well Rosencrantz and Guildenstern check in on Hamlet a lot.
*Student 2:* Yeah, that's nice. A friend checks in on you.
*Teacher:* Why would a good friend do that?
*Students: (Give an assortment of answers.)*
*Teacher:* What, of those reasons, motivate Rosencrantz and Guildenstern to check in on Hamlet?
*Student 2:* Well, none really.
*Teacher:* So, why do they? Let's use this conversation to make a list of characteristics that make a good or bad friend.

Similar conversations about the other themes yielded the following student-generated questions that are fruitful starting points when writing about theme.

## Friendship

What makes a good friend?

What is the strongest friendship in *Hamlet*?

Evaluate the friendships within *Hamlet* including Hamlet and Ophelia, Rosencrantz and Hamlet, Guildenstern and Hamlet, Horatio and Hamlet, and Marcellus and Hamlet. Which friendship is strongest? What evidence supports your evaluation? What is Shakespeare teaching us about friendship through the different relationships in *Hamlet*?

When working with the theme of friendship students have several relationships to explore that model examples and non-examples of a good friend. Rosencrantz and Guildenstern provide non-examples of friendship in that they betray Hamlet by acting as informants for Gertrude and Claudius in Act 2 Scene 2 and Act 3 Scene 1. In addition, Hamlet's treatment of Ophelia in Act 3 Scene 1 and Act 3 Scene 2 provides another non-example of a good friendship throughout their confusing and tumultuous dealings. Conversely, Horatio and Marcellus demonstrate characteristics of a good friendship. It could be argued that their desire to protect Hamlet from the ghost in Act 1 Scene 4 makes them examples of true friends. Further, Horatio, in his willingness to observe Claudius' behavior during the play in Act

3, demonstrates that he is trustworthy in Hamlet's eyes which proves his standing as a good friend. The positivity of their friendship is underscored by Horatio's final words in Act 5 Scene 2 in which he speaks tenderly and lovingly of Hamlet.

**Honesty**

Is the ghost in *Hamlet* real? What evidence in the text supports your claim?

What is the importance of honesty in a relationship?

Which characters act with the most honesty? The least?

What do you think Shakespeare may be trying to teach us about parenting in Hamlet? What evidence supports your claim?

One thread that students can follow when exploring the theme of honesty is whether or not the ghost of King Hamlet is real. Act 1 Scene 1 provides evidence that Marcellus, Bernardo, and Horatio have seen the ghost, and their experience is again confirmed by Horatio in Act 1 Scene 2. Later, their sighting is supported by Hamlet who sees the ghost in Act 1 Scene 4. Their experiences are contradicted however in Act 3 Scene 4 when the ghost of King Hamlet appears in Gertrude's chambers. Hamlet can see the ghost, but Gertrude cannot.

A second thread that students might follow concerns honesty in friendships, particularly with regards to Rosencrantz and Guildenstern. In Act 2 Scene 2 we learn that Rosencrantz and Guildenstern have been summoned and sent by Gertrude to decipher the cause behind Hamlet's mood. Since Hamlet is not present during their exchange, we can assume he does not know that they were sent by his mother. Later, in the same act and scene, Hamlet tries to get his two childhood friends to explain why they were sent to him, but they will not. Instead Hamlet tells them, and according to him it is because he no longer delights in life. In Act 3 Scene 1 Rosencrantz and Guildenstern report back to the king about Hamlet's state, and in Act 3 Scene 2 Hamlet confronts their duplicity. In Act 4 Scene 2, Hamlet again confronts their dishonesty to no effect.

Lastly, the actions and words of Claudius and Gertrude might be evaluated as a third thematic thread related to honesty. Special analytical attention should be paid to the words of advice offered to Hamlet regarding the death of his father in Act 1 Scene 2 by Gertrude and Claudius as well as their response to the play in Act 3 Scene 2. Further, the discussion between Hamlet and Gertrude in Act 3 Scene 4 as well as Claudius' confession in Act 3 Scene 3 are a treasure trove of evidence for students to mine.

**Revenge**

Evaluate the success of Claudius' revenge plan.

Is revenge a worthwhile endeavor? What evidence supports your thinking?

When wrestling with the idea of revenge students have several scenes to contemplate. Firstly in Act 1 Scene 5, Hamlet discovers that his father wants him to seek revenge for his murder. Students may argue that this must be a fantasy emerging from Hamlet's mind because surely the ghost cannot be real. The fact that Gertrude does not see the ghost when she and Hamlet meet in her chambers supports their thinking. Thus students may argue that revenge is a fantasy that we have when things do not work out the way we want them to.

Students may also argue that revenge is not worthwhile due to the outcome of Claudius and Laertes' plan in Act 5 Scene 2. Rather than ridding them of Hamlet through injury with a poisoned sword, the plan resulted in Gertrude's death as well as Hamlet and Claudius' deaths. Claudius' plan for revenge did not include losing his love Gertrude and dying himself, and thus proves the claim that revenge is not a worthwhile pursuit because if Claudius had not sought revenge he and his love might still be alive, and, one might argue, he could continue to be king.

**Parenting**

What makes a good parent?

Who is the best parent in *Hamlet*?

Evaluate the parents in *Hamlet*. Who is the best parent? What evidence supports your claim?

What do you think Shakespeare may be trying to teach us about parenting in *Hamlet*? What evidence supports your claim?

Polonius, Claudius, Gertrude, and the ghost of King Hamlet and their interactions with their children provide ample text for exploring the theme of parenting. Evidence relating to Polonius' parenting is found in Act 1 Scene 3 as he gives advice to his children, and in Act 2 Scenes 1 and 2 as he questions Ophelia about Hamlet and then reports back to Claudius and Gertrude. These scenes may lead students to contemplate the role of trust within a parent and child relationship. Evidence of Claudius and Gertrude's parenting is plentiful as their relationship with Hamlet is central to the story, but there are text gems in Act 1 Scene 2 in Claudius' advice to Hamlet in which he advises Hamlet to simply accept his father's death and in Act 3 Scene 4 in which Hamlet and Gertrude argue. Lastly, it is interesting to have students reflect on the ghost. The ghost is, of course, Hamlet's father who commands Hamlet to seek revenge. Would a good parent expect their child to seek revenge? Evaluating the parenting choices of characters' insights can lead to intense discussion among students.

## *Romeo and Juliet*

### Conflict and Violence

How should conflicts be resolved?

What makes conflicts difficult to resolve?

When considering the topic of conflict and violence, students frequently argue that within *Romeo and Juliet*, Shakespeare is trying to teach us that violence, rather than solving conflict, actually only makes conflict worse. There is evidence of this throughout the play. In Act 1 Scene 1, the reader learns that the play is about two families in conflict, immediately after a giant fight breaks out in the street. Fighting in the street resolves nothing. Rather, their physical violence makes the situation worse as the prince ends the conflict by threatening to end the life of those who next bring violence to Verona's streets. Later, in Act 1 Scene 5 Tybalt notices Romeo, his family's enemy, at his uncle Lord Capulet's party. Tybalt wants to use violence to chase Romeo and his friends away, however, his uncle urges Tybalt to keep the peace, and so he does. Here, students may even make the point that a happy party is more likely to bring enemies to peace than a street fight, and in that way maintaining peace and being happy together has more power to resolve conflicts than resorting to violence. In contrast to the earlier scene, and as a result of his dissuading

Tybalt from resorting to violence, Lord Capulet's party happens without incident. In Act 3 Scene 1, however, we see further evidence of how violence exacerbates conflict rather than resolving it, when Tybalt seeks out Romeo to get back at him for attending the party. In this scene Tybalt ends up killing Romeo's friend and getting killed himself which results in Romeo's banishment. Again, we see violence creating more problems and solving none. Students can continue to pursue this argument to the final scenes of the drama in which Romeo and Juliet resort to the most final of all violence – suicide – to resolve their problems. And, although we can presume their final acts bring peace to the feuding families, that peace comes with piles of grief which bring new problems for the families to cope with.

**Love and Friendship**
What makes a good friend or girl/boyfriend?

When exploring themes of friendship and love in *Romeo and Juliet*, considering what, according to Shakespeare, makes a good friend, girlfriend, or boyfriend, can lead students to compelling thesis statements about theme. Most often students focus on loyalty and honesty as the key ingredients, however when seeking evidence to support either idea, they struggle. This provides an opportunity to teach students that theme is about what the author is trying to teach us about a topic of subject, not what we as readers think. While students may feel that honesty and loyalty are key factors, Shakespeare may not have been speaking on those topics specifically, which is why locating evidence is challenging. Thus, we must carefully consider what the text is actually saying as we wonder what Shakespeare was trying to teach the reader about love. When recentering the question around Shakespeare's intended message rather than the reader's opinion on the topic, students get closer to establishing a theme that can be supported with text evidence. For instance, it could be argued that a good friend's love is deep and loyal and not shallow. Evidence for this thematic claim might lie in an example and non-example. A non-example can be found in Romeo's relationship with Rosaline. When we meet Romeo he is devastated that his love for Rosaline is unrequited. He seems obsessed with her, yet a brief time later he meets Juliet and is absolutely obsessed with her instead, and

Rosaline disappears. Romeo's quick flip of love interests suggests that his feelings are shallow since they can be changed so quickly. Thus, Romeo's feelings for Juliet cannot be categorized as love because there is no depth to his feelings. On the other hand, an example of a good friend's love being deep and loyal is in Act 3 Scene 1 where Romeo kills Tybalt, after Tybalt kills Mercutio. Mercutio was only in conflict with Tybalt because he was standing up to Tybalt on Romeo's behalf. Since Romeo was not defending himself, Mercutio stepped in to do so for his friend. In response, Romeo retaliated against Tybalt on behalf of his friend. This example shows us that a good friend is willing to go to great lengths to protect and defend loved ones, just as Romeo and Mercutio did for one another. Now, some students use this same evidence to argue a different theme entirely, which is absolutely fine! As long as students use sound reasoning and evidence to support their thinking they have the agency to argue any claim they find compelling.

**Decision Making**

How do our decisions affect ourselves and others in unexpected ways?

One theme related to decision making that students often argue is that decisions can lead to unintended consequences. Throughout Romeo and Juliet are characters making decisions that lead to unwanted results, much like students in our own classrooms who tease and instigate until a larger conflict breaks out, only then to claim: "We were just kidding around!" Sampson, Gregory, Abraham, Tybalt, and Benvolio do not anticipate that the conflict they carelessly engaged in in Act 1 Scene 1 would provoke the Prince to escalate punishment to the stage where further violence would result in the banishment of Romeo. In Act 2 Scene 3 when the Friar agrees to marry Romeo and Juliet, he thinks he will be bringing the chance for peace between the Montagues and Capulets, which does occur, but not without the unintended consequence of Romeo and Juliet's death. One might argue that Tybalt is protecting the honor of his family by fighting Romeo in Act 3 Scene 1, however the outcome of that decision is the unintended death of Mercutio and Tybalt himself. Similar evidence can be found in an examination of decisions made by Juliet's nurse and parents.

A second decision-related theme relates to maturity and the question of how much control adults should have over young people's decision making. Or, to what degree are young people mature enough to make their own decisions? There are several text points that students might refer to when exploring this theme. First, Act 1 Scene 1 shows a group of Romeo's peers unable to avoid a conflict. Then in Act 2 Romeo falls in love with Juliet after having just been in love with Rosaline. Later in the act Romeo and Juliet decide to get married after knowing each other for less than a week. In Act 3 Scene 3 Romeo pouts after being banished from Verona for killing Tybalt. Romeo fails to see that being banished is far less a punishment than being killed. These scenes in the text demonstrate that the characters are intensely motivated by their own wants and emotions which one could argue makes them immature and incapable of making the best decisions for themselves. Mercutio's Queen Mab speech in Act 1 Scene 4 underscores this theme as it reminds the reader of how young people are driven by dreams more than logic and reason.

**FIGURE 4.1** Surrounded by the setting for *A Midsummer Night's Dream*, a student contemplates theme.

Note: In this chapter, an engraving of Shakespeare's face by Charles Droeshout (1623) has been used to protect children's identities in photographs.

## *A Midsummer Night's Dream*

### Love and Friendship

What makes a good friend or girl/boyfriend?

What obstacles can prevent good relationships from forming?

One theme related to love and friendship that students have discussed concerns the obstacles that one must overcome in order to form loving relationships. Students often identify jealousy as one of the primary obstacles, however there are a variety of other obstacles that they recognize as well including parental commands and other people's meddling. In the text we see the effects of jealousy on relationship in Helena's conversation with Hermia at the end of Act 1 Scene 1 and in the exchange between Helena and Demetrius in Act 1 Scene 2. Text related to the theme of meddling in relationships is seen throughout the play as Oberon and Puck intervene. Their intervention initially keeps the lovers apart, so it is an obstacle to their relationship. Finally, Egeus, Hermia's father, commands his daughter to obey his wishes with regards to who she marries which creates an obstacle in her relationship with her father and with Lysander, the boy she wants to marry, but whom her father disapproves of. Egeus' command creates an obstacle for both his relationship with his daughter, and for his daughter's relationship with Lysander. Obstacles are also seen in Oberon and Titania's relationship in which an unresolved conflict in Act 2 Scene 1 leads to revenge on Oberon's part in Act 3 Scene 1. Conflict and revenge are definite obstacles to relationships! Indeed, the course of true love does not run smoothly.

### Activity 1: Object Reflection

In order to encourage the abstract thinking necessary to determine theme, it is helpful to warm up with this more complex version of show and tell (O'Neil & Lambert, 1982). In object reflections, students choose an object that symbolically answers an essential question related to theme. Question ideas for each story discussed in this text are presented following the lesson steps. In my experience, such questions can be organically inferred or even pulled directly from student-generated questions during a prior close read of the text. Students will most likely need time to reflect and select their objects before sharing, so plan on discussing the assignment one day, and actually doing the activity on another day.

**Time:** One class session, plus time before to discuss the assignment with students so they have time to gather objects.

**Materials:** Objects that students select and bring from home!

**Steps:**

1. Discuss the general definition of theme with students as the answer to this question: In one word, what is the story about, and what advice about life is the author giving you on that topic? Explain that prior to thinking about what Shakespeare's advice about life's themes are, they are going to explore their own ideas about the meaning of some of life's big themes.
2. Post one or several open-ended thematic questions for students to contemplate. Direct them to select one if more than one question was posted.
3. Students complete a reflective quick write on the question assigned or selected. Then, they should consider what object to bring in that would symbolize their thinking. For instance, when responding to the question "What makes a good father?" a student once brought in Band-Aids. Their reasoning was that a good father should be able to take care of and help heal the hurts of life. Another student brought in a jersey to answer the question about what makes a good friend because they wanted to express the idea that a friend is always on your team, or on your side rooting for you.
4. When students have gathered their objects and brought them to class, conduct a sharing session in which students present their thinking. One option for sharing is to split the class in half. Have one half make an outer circle, and the other half make an inner circle facing the outer circle. The inner circle of students rotate every few minutes to create a new sharing partnership. As students share they should be responsible for collecting three new ideas from their classmates. A debrief in which student ideas are collected on a theme web poster

will hold students accountable as well as capture their initial thinking for later theme work and discussion.
5. To add complexity to this assignment it is interesting for students to consider how different characters might respond to this same activity. Have students pretend that Romeo, or Ophelia, or Helena etc., are given the same assignment, and consider how they might respond. For instance, if contemplating the question of friendship, Tybalt might bring in a sword to symbolize the importance of physical protection in relationships.

## A Midsummer Night's Dream

What does it take to be a good friend?
   What does it take to be a good boyfriend/girlfriend?
   Is it more important to take care of our own needs or the needs of others first?

## Romeo and Juliet

When is a young person ready for independence?
   What does it take to be a good boyfriend/girlfriend?
   What is true love? And, do you think Romeo and Juliet are truly in love?

## Hamlet

What makes a good father?
   Is revenge worthwhile?
   What is the importance of honesty?

### Activity 2: Advice Vlogs or Blogs

An important reading skill for students to develop in order to identify theme is recognizing points at which characters are making decisions. When a character makes a decision, it clues the reader into whether or not the character is growing and changing and alerts the reader to pay attention to possible plot twists. Noticing how a character is changing leads students to identify what is being learned, which, in turn, illuminates the theme of the text for the reader. By pausing at the points where a character makes a choice to consider what the reader thinks the character should do, and then comparing that to what they actually do, the reader is cultivating an inner sense of theme as well as working towards understanding the character's motivation.

**Time:** One to two class periods.
**Materials:**

- Supplies for writing letters or emails, etc.
- Envelopes.

**Steps:**

1. Write a letter, email, blog, carrier pigeon note, etc., from one character to a wise advisor. The character's letter should explain the situation as well. There are situation suggestions at the end of this lesson.
2. The return letter should advise the character and evaluate their thinking.
3. Students might debrief this lesson through a series of whole class sharing activities or an informal piece of writing in which students reflect on what the advice letters reveal abut theme.

## A Midsummer Night's Dream

Throughout the play the love matches among Hermia, Lysander, Helena, and Demetrius are continually shifting. First, Helena is upset that she is not as beautiful as Hermia and that is why Demetrius does not love her. This also puts Hermia in an uncomfortable position as she must confront her friend's jealousy. Then because of Puck and Oberon's meddling, Lysander falls in love with Helena, which creates conflict between the friends. Each of these predicaments, and those that follow, would be an excellent point at which to ask for advice.

## Romeo and Juliet

In Act 2 Scene 3 Romeo visits Father Lawrence. Romeo is experiencing a person versus society conflict in that he wants to marry

Juliet but the feud between their families will not allow home to ask for her hand directly. In this same scene Father Lawrence is conflicted too. His is a person versus self conflict, as he wonders whether or not he should marry them. A third perspective to consider might be Rosaline. What internal conflicts might she be feeling when she finds out about Romeo and Juliet's marriage?

## Hamlet

One of the central conflicts to *Hamlet* is the idea of revenge and Hamlet's person versus self conflict and struggle to decide whether or not to seek revenge and follow the commands of his ghost father. Should Hamlet seek revenge? If not, what action should he take?

### Activity 3: Theme Reflection Journals

There are several reflective strategies that can be used when students are working to decipher theme. Each of these activities can be completed by the class as a whole, or they can be jigsawed in order to maximize student exposure to these strategies for determining theme.

**Repeating Symbolism** – This journal entry is based on a strategy from Lehman and Roberts (2014). They explain that authors often repeatedly insert imagery, objects, or other elements into a story to emphasize the theme. Looking for repetition can help students uncover theme if they identify repeating symbolism and work to determine the possible meaning.

Each member of the team should select an act to reread. As you reread, keep an eye out for any repeating symbols or images. After, reading and annotating listen to your peer's analysis. Did they discuss any images or symbols that you noticed in your reading? Why repeating symbolism did your team find? What do you think the meaning of these symbols are? Why did the author repeat them? What do they reveal about the theme?

**Character Self Talk** – According to Beers and Probst (2012), often, when characters are reflecting out loud to themselves, or when their thinking is made known to the reader through their thoughts, the topic of their reflection relates to the theme of the story. So, in examining a character's words to themselves, clues about theme can be unearthed.

Each member of the team should select an act to reread. As you reread, keep an eye out for any character self-talk. After, reading and annotating listen to your peer's analysis. What characters had moments of self-talk? What were they telling themselves in those moments? What do you think their self-talk reveals about the theme?

**Character Change** – Most stories are stories of a change that occurs within the main character. In noting how a character was at the beginning of a story relative to who they are at the end can help readers determine what lesson was learned, and thus the theme of the story (Seravallo, 2015).

Each member of the team should select a major character to focus on. As you reread, keep an eye out for any changes within characters. It might be helpful to annotate any important choices the character makes. After, reading and annotating listen to your peer's analysis. What differences did you note in the character from the beginning of the text to the end? What changes within the character's beliefs or actions? Why did this change occur? What does the change within the character reveal about the theme?

**Wise Advice** – The role of secondary characters is often to teach the main character(s) or to help them come to understand something important about life. Examining the text to identify areas in which a secondary character instructs a main character about an important fact of life can also illuminate theme (Beers & Proust, 2012).

Each member of the team should select a minor character to focus on. As you reread, keep an eye out for any instances where the minor character gives the major character advice. Annotate any points in the story where this occurs. After, reading and annotating listen to your peer's analysis. What advice did you note was being given from one minor character to another character? What might this advice reveal about the theme?

**Time:** One to four class periods plus additional time for debrief and sharing.

**Materials:** Something to be used as a theme journal where essential elements about student findings, as determined by the class and or teacher, are recorded will be needed. This might be a digital document, a slideshow, a blank notebook, or sketchbook.

**Steps:**

1. Students individually or within teams decide which journal to do.
2. Within teams students consider the prompt for the type of journal they would like to do, reread and annotate the text according to the journal prompt.
3. Teams share and discuss their annotations and explain how they relate to the prompt.
4. Finally, within teams or individually students do either a reflective quick write, a sketch note, or a chart to show their thinking before sharing out with the whole group or with another team.

## Considerations

Working with theme is an excellent opportunity to incorporate philosophy. David A. White's book *Philosophy for Kids* (2001) identifies key questions raised by philosophers across history and provides a brief lesson and discussion questions related to the question at hand. Alternately, a google search for lessons related to these philosophers yields a trove of options.

### Love and Friendship

Aristotle had a lot to say about friendship. Specifically he argued that friendship requires three things: Good will between two people, a wish for continued good will based on usefulness, pleasure, or moral goodness, and a knowledge of good will being mutual (White, 2001). A brief exploration of Aristotle's philosophy of friendship can help students think about the idea of friendship more abstractly which will prepare them to apply their own ideas and discuss the theme more broadly. It would be interesting to hear a conversation between Helena, Hermia, and Aristotle! Or between Mercutio and Romeo!

## Honesty

Immanuel Kant's philosophical musings deal with the complexities of lying and whether or not it is ever justified. He argued that a lie was never justified because a lie always damages the truth and creates a confusion about what is right and wrong. According to Kant, the ends do not justify the means (White, 2001). In other words, even if we are lying to create a good and fair outcome, it is not acceptable to lie to achieve that positive outcome. How would a conversation between Kant and Claudius play out? What would Tybalt have to say in response to Kant?

## Violence as a Solution

Dr. Martin Luther King Jr's life and philosophy was based on the idea that violence is never an acceptable means to achieving social justice (White, 2001). I wonder how Dr. King would feel about Hamlet's choice not to kill Claudius as he prayed, or how Dr. King might have intervened had he stumbled across the Montague and Capulets' street brawls.

## Existence

In his famous soliloquy which begins, "to be or not to be" Hamlet contemplates whether existence is worthwhile. Similarly, Rene Descartes grappled with this question. He came to the conclusion that one cannot question that they exist if they are thinking that they exist in the first place (White, 2001). He coined the famous phrase, "I think therefore, I am." While Descartes is not questioning the worthiness of existence, but rather how one knows they exist, certainly he and Hamlet would have an interesting exchange about the concept what is means to be a living human being.

## Perception versus Reality

The dream motif in *A Midsummer Night's Dream* certainly entangles itself among philosophical questions related to how we perceive the world versus how the world actually is. Bertrand Russel argued that what is real allows for data to be collected by the senses (White, 2001). However, this argument begs to be discussed as is does not account for the fact that sensory data that we collect is interpreted individually. For instance, a sound that is soothing to one person can be grating to another, thus what is the actual reality of the sound being hear by both individuals.

## Revisiting Essential Unit Question

### What Is the Power of Language?

As discussed earlier, theme is important to humans because it allows us to see patterns and communicate lessons for better living to each other across time. How would humanity be different if we did not use story to teach lessons over time? During this discussion of the essential question students might consider the teachings and thinking of different philosophers to arrive at more abstract and complex ideas to add to the essential question web. Such ideas might be revealed by a brief research period in which students hunt for other philosopher's thoughts on the theme being discussed.

## Resources

This text is an excellent starting point for exploring philosophy in the classroom in conjunction with Shakespeare or as a standalone exploration!

White, D. (2001). *Philosophy for Kids: 40 Fun Questions That Help You Wonder About Everything!* Routledge.

## References

Beers, K., & Proust, R. (2012). *Notice and note: Strategies for close reading.* Heinemann.

Lamb, C. & Lamb, M. (1807). *Tales from Shakespeare.* Juvenile Library of William Godwin.

Lehman, C., & Roberts, K. (2014). *Falling in love with close reading: Lessons for analyzing texts and life.* Heinemann.

National Governors Association Center for Best Practices & Council of Chief State School Officers. (2010). *Common core state standards for English language arts and literacy in history/social studies, science, and technical subjects.*

O'Neil, C., & Lambert, A. (1982). *Drama structures: A practical handbook for teachers*. Heinemann.

Smith, M. W., & Wilhelm, J. D. (2010). *Fresh takes on teaching literary elements*. Scholastic Teaching Resources.

Serravallo, J. (2015). *The reading strategies book: Your everything guide to developing skilled readers with 300 strategies*. Heinemann.

Shakespeare, W. (1596). *A midsummer night's dream*.

Shakespeare, W. (1597). *Romeo and Juliet*.

Shakespeare, W. (1601). *Hamlet*.

# 5
# Vocabulary and Word Choice

A common struggle when working with a text is how to approach vocabulary instruction. We wonder which words to focus on, which to teach during a interactive read aloud, which to have students record definitions and so on. The routine I have found most successful was to have students focus on highlighting unknown or unfamiliar words during the first reading of the text as described in the close read routine of Chapter 3. Then, students record their words on sticky notes and sort their words into one of three word wall posters (Harper, 2016) The first poster is level one and is for words that the students think they already know, but just want to be sure. Level two is for words students have heard, but do not know the meaning. The level three poster is for words that are entirely unfamiliar to the students. These posters serve as starting points for students as they select words to study.

Seeing these words sorted in this manner helps me determine a couple important things. One, every text has words that must be understood in order to understand the text as a whole. For instance, in *Hamlet* the concept of a court is necessary to appreciate the relationship dynamics that lead to betrayals. It is the atmosphere at court that contributes to Hamlet's behavior. A wide and fairly deep sense of the meaning of the word court contributes to a greater understanding of the text. When working with Shakespeare, the exception to the rule that students drive the selection of words, is with regards to crucial words that have changed drastically in meaning since Shakespeare was born, or in words like court that are essential to a deeper understanding of the text. Two, the sorted word posters help me see how much time we need to spend on vocabulary, and how that time needs to be spent. If there are many words in the level three poster, words students identify as being unfamiliar, then I know that letting students loose on self-selected vocabulary word journals may need to wait until some direct vocabulary instruction and discussion happens. On the other hand, if there are more words on the level one and two posters then I know the kids might be ready to have more immediate agency in their selection and study of words.

Do not stress yourself with trying to develop a comprehensive list of vocabulary words in Shakespeare's works that will be unfamiliar to your students. Nearly all of them will, and therein lies magic. Shakespeare is full of reading riddles. There are moments when reading Shakespeare may feel like you are reading a foreign language successfully, and then suddenly, you're lost. That experience can create motivation to figure out the Bard's code – if the teacher brings an attitude of co-discovery and persistence. Focus words can be determined after one read through in which the students become agents of their own vocabulary development. If kids are not collecting the words, their level of engagement and commitment to learning will be diminished.

This chapter meets the needs of learners as they develop a deeper vocabulary and work to understand the importance of Greek and Latin to the development of the English language. Beginning with the idea that Shakespeare is responsible for creating words that we use today, this unit includes a project that allows students to develop their knowledge of Greek and Latin roots. By combining those roots and other word parts to be like Shakespeare, they create words that are made up, but have a definition related to the root they contain. Other activities include developing a visual metaphor for how the English language was created and general activities for vocabulary development that can be used throughout the unit.

## Learning Goals

The goal of determining the meaning of words and phrases used in the text is the same for students working from lower to higher levels of vocabulary development.

Stating learning goals directly will help students identify the purpose of instruction and thus be more likely to achieve it. Specifically, students will grow in their ability to identify the meaning of unknown words. This can be stated as follows for students: "I can use different strategies to figure out the meaning of unknown words as I read." Additionally, students will grow their own personal vocabularies as they select and study words themselves. This learning goal can be stated for students as: I can develop my own vocabulary by choosing specific words to study.

### Module Learning Goals

| | Going Far | | | | |
|---|---|---|---|---|---|
| | 4 | 5 | 6 | 7 | 8 |
| | Determine meaning of words and phrases used in the text. The learning goal is the same across grade levels, so students can go far by choosing: To increase the number of words studied. To study words at or above a certain syllable count. To produce original writing using a set number of words. To learn a certain amount of words within a period of time. To teach the class a certain amount of words within a period of time. | | | | |
| | Fluency | | Word choice impacts meaning and tone. | | |
| | Going Deep | | | | |
| | I learned and can apply ten Greek and/or Latin roots to understanding new words. | | | | |
| | I kept a personal word journal of words I would like to include in my own vocabulary. | | | | |
| | I created a piece of writing that correctly uses ten words in my word journal. | | | | |
| | I annotated my script to show which words I will emphasize to communicate the tone I want my character to have in various scenes. | | | | |

The benchmarks for this learning goal were established using the Common Core Standards.

## Instruction: Assessments

Assessments for this module can take several forms. Most simply, a text dependent question related to vocabulary, and based on a specific passage that asks students to explain the meaning of a specific word as it related to the passage can assess strategies practiced throughout the word journal activities. Question prompt ideas are provided after each word journal style.

A simple question stem that provides a text dependent question framework is this:

> What is the meaning of the word _____ as it is used in the text on line _____ ? Explain how you know the meaning of the word.

## Instruction: Learning Activities

These can be used in conjunction with close reads, as students build comprehension, or they can be used on their own if vocabulary development is the desired focus. In either case, it is best to do these activities with words the students have identified.

### Activity 1: Vocabulary Skits

Vocabulary skits are student-created 60-second performances that are quickly prepared and often very funny. The purpose of the skit is for the team to use their word as many times as possible with in a 60-second time limit. The activity is based on research that suggests our brain needs us to use a word 7–15 times before it becomes part of our long-term memory and functional vocabulary, thus the repetition (Lawrence, 2009; McKeown, Beck, Omanson, & Pople 1985; Nagy, Herman, & Anderson, 1985). This activity also acclimates students to performing in front of an audience.

**Time:** This activity takes approximately 30 minutes as described but can be shortened or lengthened depending on the number of words and teams involved.

**Materials:**

- Vocabulary list posters that feature words identified as new or challenging by students should be posted. The posters should have space for the word and for the definition as the word is used in the text so that the posters can become sources of support while reading the text. It is helpful to have the lists separated by act and sorted alphabetically. This can be accomplished most easily if students add words to the posters on sticky notes as they read each act. Within the Lamb texts tildes designate the end of one act and the start of the next to facilitate this process.
- Lamb texts.
- Word maps.
- Timer.
- Word study tools such as an online dictionary and thesaurus.

**Steps:**

1. Divide students into teams of three or four. Distribute a word web to each student and assign a word to each team. Instruct individual students to complete their web using whatever resources necessary: Online dictionary, thesaurus, the text. After several minutes, have students share their webs with their teams to reach consensus on acceptable answers. Students should make corrections as necessary.
2. Once the teacher has seen evidence that teams have a sound understanding of their word, including its variations, students are ready to create their skits. Skits can be silly and funny and absurd. The most important thing is that the students use the word correctly and in all of its variations without just repeating it over and over. It is helpful to quickly circulate to make sure teams have a solid scenario before they get too far along. Give students a minute to get their idea and scenario together, or assign specific scenarios if students need support. Recording skits and having students quickly evaluate their skit prior to performing in front of the class is highly instructive. In watching their playback, students can

identify and correct improper usage, imagine additional ways to include their word, and practice correct pronunciation.
3. Students take turns sharing their skits. Before performing, the team shares their web to teach the word to the class. Students may add words to their word study notebooks as their peers present. Then, after assigning the timing duty to one student allow the team to perform. Invite students to count correct usage examples as the skit is being performed. At the end of the skit, have the class reach consensus on how many correct usage of the assigned word the skit contained. It can be fun to make this a competition with a silly award being given to the team with the most correct usage examples contained in their skit.
4. An assessment for this activity might require students to complete an exit ticket related to the words studied through the skits during that class session.

## Activity 2: Personal Word Journals

Personal word journals are notebooks that contain information that students record about words they want to learn more about. During a close read students can collect unfamiliar or infrequently used words to add to their journals. Word journal time can be a regularly occurring segment of the class period, and journal styles can be assigned, or self-selected by students. To maintain interest and novelty, it is helpful to allow students to rotate word journal types at regular intervals. A wise decision would be to save time for students to share their findings at the conclusion of each word journal session to extend student learning via informal peer to peer instruction.

**Time:** A regularly occurring 10–20-minute block of time
**Materials:**

- Word journals.
- Lamb or Shortened Shakespeare text with unfamiliar or infrequently used words important to the individual student highlighted.
- Word study tools such as an online dictionary and thesaurus.
- Timer.

## Formats

**Humor and Multiple Meanings:** Shakespeare is known for using words with multiple meanings to bring humor to his work. Often, the word is repeated as a homophone or homograph. In this type of word journal, students research the various meanings of the words they selected, and then return to the text to identify the definition being used in the text. This word journal type was inspired by Jennifer Serravallo's Multiple Meaning Words strategy as described in her reading strategies book (Serravallo, 2015).

**Close Read Prompt:** Read the passage to identify words that Shakespeare may have chosen to use because of the humor created by its multiple meanings. Choose one example to explain.

## Examples of Humorous Multiple Meanings Words
### A Midsummer Night's Dream

- In Act 1 Scene 2 we meet Bottom, who provides the most enjoyable experience of Shakespeare's use of double meanings to bring humor. Bottom is of course later turned into a donkey, or ass, which is a hilarious choice of Shakespeare's considering how stubborn, bossy, and arrogant he shows himself to be during the Mechanicals' rehearsals.
- In Act 2 Scene 1, Demetrius and Helena are arguing. They each used the word sick to describe the way they feel about each other, but it is clear they do not mean the word in the same sense which creates another humorous exchange.

### Romeo and Juliet

- In Act 1 Scene 4, Mercutio is trying to persuade Romeo to dance once they enter the Capulet's party. Romeo replies that he cannot dance because it is Mercutio who actually has the "nimble soles," whereas Romeo feels he has "a soul of led." This use of the homonyms sole and soul creates a pun.
- Later, Mercutio and Romeo are discussing their dreams and when asked what his dream was, Mercutio says "That dreamers often lie." To which Romeo responds, "In bed asleep." This creates a humorous moment because of the dual meanings of lie.

- Again the word "lie" appears with more than one meaning applying in Act 2 Scene 3. In this scene Romeo is visiting Friar Lawrence. Friar Lawrence warns him that young men's love then lies not truly in their hearts, but in their eyes. Not only is Friar Lawrence telling Romeo that young men often fall in love only based on the shallowness of looks, but often their love tells lies. Given the fact that this advice is given in the middle of a conversation about how quickly Romeo fell out of love with Rosaline, it seems that the Friar is warning him that his heart may not be truthful to Juliet.

## Hamlet

- In Act 1 Scene 2 Hamlet describes Claudius as, "A little more than kin, but less than kind." The play on the words kin and kind illuminates Hamlet's sense of humor, and reveals his feelings about Claudius. We would expect kin to be kind, but as Hamlet points out Claudius is definitely not kind.
- Act 3 Scene 2 finds Hamlet engaged in conversation with Polonius. When discussing his acting experience Polonius says, "I was killed in the Capitol; Brutus killed me." Hamlet replies, "it was a brute part of him to kill so capital a calf." While Polonius thinks Hamlet is making another odd remark, we know that Shakespeare would not have repeated those words unless there was an intentional second meaning. The play on Brutus and brute is clear, brute comes from brutal and this is Hamlet seizing an opportunity to call Claudius and Polonius brutal for their role in murdering and supporting the murder of King Hamlet. Capitol in Polonius' usage refers to Rome where Caesar was killed by those he thought were his friends, including the traitorous Brutus. Hamlet's use of the word capital in response to Polonius is another slight as in this form the word means most important or highest ranking. The capital calf Hamlet is referring to is his father, the king. Hamlet is using a play on Polonius' own words to insult him and Claudius. Later, in the same scene, Hamlet uses the word play multiple times in conversation with both Rosencrantz and Guildenstern to the same effect.

**Word! That's Your Job:** We can often tell the meaning of an unknown word by analyzing the job it is doing in a sentence. Most often a word's job is related to its part of speech. In this word journal, students analyze the word by asking themselves what job the word is doing, by looking at surrounding words to determine the relationships and context, to finally arrive at meaning. This word journal is based on strategies presented in the book *No More "Look Up the List" Vocabulary Instruction* (Cobb & Blachowicz, 2014).

**Close Read Prompt:** Read the passage to identify unfamiliar words that Shakespeare chose to use. What is the job the word is doing in the sentence? Is it describing something? What is being described? How is it being described?

### Examples of Unfamiliar Words
*A Midsummer Night's Dream*

In Act 2 Scene 2 Titania is preparing to sleep and giving her fairy helpers directions. She says, "Come, now a roundel and a fairy song; Then, for the third part of a minute, hence;". After these words she sends some fairies to take care of rose buds, and others she sends to war with bats for their wings. In this passage the word hence is strange and unclear to students. Considering its job may bring clarity if students consider what comes right after – Titania is giving orders. So, the job of the word must have something to do with the command to go and do. A dictionary double check confirms this thinking.

*Romeo and Juliet*

In Act 1 Scene 2 Benvolio is persuading Romeo to enter the Capulet's party so that he can compare all the beauties of Verona to Rosaline. He commands Romeo to "Go thither." In this case students can infer through context and questioning what the word thither must mean: In here or over there. Essentially it is referring to a place that Romeo should go. In this situation, it is the Capulets' party.

In Act 2 Scene 1 Juliet declares one of her most famous lines: "O Romeo, Romeo! Wherefore art thou Romeo?" Many people think that Juliet is asking where Romeo is, but that is inaccurate. One clue that can lead students to the correct meaning of "wherefore" is the context of the second line: "Deny thy father and refuse thy name." The command to "refuse thy name" tells the readers that Juliet isn't asking where Romeo is, but *why* is Romeo, as in Romeo Montague. She is asking why he has to be a Montague, and she wonders why he can't just refuse his name. So, "wherefore" means why or for what reason, not "where" as in "where are you?"

## Hamlet

In Act 1 Scene 1 Bernardo tells Horatio, "Looks it not like the king? Mark it, Horatio." They are guarding Elsinore and have seen the ghost. The word "mark" may be odd for students to see in this situation. They might ask themselves what job the word is doing. The student's inner dialogue may sound like this: Bernardo is asking if the ghost looks like the king. Is he asking Horatio to put a mark or scribble on the ghost? No, that would be silly. Were markers even invented yet? It seems like Bernardo may be asking Horatio to look carefully or to pay attention to what Bernardo said.

**Moods and Meanings:** Words can be mysterious in the sense that they can convey feeling or mood within the reader without the reader necessarily knowing exactly what the word means, so sometimes it can be helpful to reflect on how words make us feel to determine meaning. In a mood and meaning word journal, students record context clues related to mood, as well as their own reflection on what mood the author's words evoke in the readers and characters. This word journal type was inspired by Jennifer Serravallo's Multiple Meaning Words strategy as described in her reading strategies book (Serravallo, 2015).

**Close Read Prompt:** Read the passage to identify words that Shakespeare may have chosen to use because of the mood it creates.

## Examples of Words that Create Mood
### *A Midsummer Night's Dream*

In Act 2 Scene 1 we the reader spy on Demetrius and Helena's argument just as Oberon is – unseen. Demetrius is telling Helena to leave him alone because he does not love her. However, an undeterred Helena compares herself to a dog in her love for Demetrius. She tells him she is a spaniel and uses the words beat, spurn, strike, neglect, lose, unworthy, and beg to describe what she is willing to tolerate for his love. These words create a mood of discomfort for the reader, and punishment for Helena. This mood is created to show the reader the unhealthy extremes Helena is willing to go to be loved by Demetrius.

### *Romeo and Juliet*

In the middle of Act 1 Scene 1 the Prince gives a monologue to the brawling Montagues and Capulets. We know he is angry, but it is the words Shakespeare used in the monologue that creates the mood that swirls around his anger: rebellious, enemies, profaners, fire, rage, torture, bloody, and weapons. To say the Prince's speech is intense is an understatement. In creating such a strong mood, Shakespeare is underscoring the danger the families are in and increases the dramatic tension for the reader.

There is a magical mood created during Romeo's famous "But soft…" monologue. In it his use of the words light, sun, moon, stars, heaven, twinkle, brightness, and others create a mural of celestial imagery in the reader's mind.

### *Hamlet*

In Scene 1, at guard outside Elsinore, Horatio uses the words harrows, fear, wonder, and warlike. He is described as trembling and pale by Bernardo. These words help create the mood of fright and suspense in the darkness surrounding the castle as the guards await the appearance of the ghost.

In Act 4 Scene 7 Queen Gertrude must explain to Laertes that his sister Ophelia died in an accident while playing next to the river. Before delivering the news, she describes Ophelia's play on the flowering river bank by using the following words: Aslant, cold, dead men's fingers, envious, weeping brook, and distress. These words create a different mood than one might expect of a girl playing in flowers next to a river.

**Phunky Phrases:** Shakespeare's writing is full of complex phrasing in which students might encounter several connected and unfamiliar words. In this case, students should be encouraged to attack the entire phrase. Such phrases are often examples of figurative language, so the presence of a figurative language reference chart is helpful to have posted for student reference. When analyzing phrases, students should consider the job the phrase is doing, the meaning of each word within the phrase, and its figurative meaning.

**Close Read Prompt:** Read the passage to identify complex phrases that Shakespeare used. Then consider the phrase as a whole and attack it word by word to determine the meaning.

## Examples of Complex Phrases
### *A Midsummer Night's Dream*

In Act 1 Scene 1 Hippolyta uses the phrase, "Four days will quickly steep themselves in night." She is speaking to Theseus about the fact that they will be getting married in four days. Once placed in context, and analyzed for unknown words, students will realize that steep is the only unfamiliar word. Being an avid tea drinker, I would demonstrate steeping for students with an actual tea bag, but a simple google search or dictionary inquiry will show students that the meaning of the word is to soak in liquid so as to extract. So, now the question is how and why would days be soaked like teabags? Hippolyta is saying that the days will transform by steeping themselves in night. She uses a beautiful image to tell us that the time until the wedding will pass quickly.

In Act 1 Scene 4, Horatio is trying to discourage Romeo from following the ghost. He warns Hamlet that the ghost may "deprive your sovereignty of reason." By investigating and using tools to define each individual word, students can surmise that the phrase means to take away one's ability to freely think and be reasonable.

## Romeo and Juliet

During Act 1 Scene 4 Romeo explains the dream he had that included a "vile forfeit of untimely death." Students may begin to unravel the meaning in this phrase by starting with the word forfeit as they may have experienced it in the context of sports. To forfeit is to give up, but as in punishment. Vile is something gross and evil, so a vile forfeit is a gross punishment. In this case Shakespeare tells us exactly what the punishment is: untimely death. That is death that is not on time. Deconstructing this phrase also leads students to understand that through Romeo's words, Shakespeare is foreshadowing the tragedy to come.

As Mercutio is dying in Act 3 Scene 1 he shouts, "A plague on both your houses…" to Romeo and Tybalt. It seems that Mercutio is putting a curse on the Capulets and Montagues through Tybalt and Romeo. The word that gives the phrase the feeling of a curse is the word plague. Students may have a sense that a plague is not a good thing if they don't know the specific meaning of the word. This is enough to understand the gist of what Mercutio is saying, though further investigation as to the meaning of plague will illuminate the degree of Mercutio's rage. He is not wishing an itchy rash or sniffly nose. He is calling for the utter destruction of their families. The word houses can be connected to the Prologue in which students might recall that households was synonymous with the entire family – including servants. Mercutio is cursing Tybalt and Romeo's families because he blames them for his death.

## Hamlet

At the end of Act 3 Scene 1, Ophelia, who has just returned Hamlet's love letters to him, says, "Rich gifts wax poor when givers prove unkind." While each of these words may be familiar to students, the meaning of the phrase may take an extra moment of reflection to decipher. The word they'd be least familiar with – wax – may need to be investigated to understand that wax can refer to a product made by bees to fashion candles, but it can also mean to increase in power as with a moon growing full. Putting this knowledge together with the phrase leads students to understand that this phrase means that the value of a gift decreases when it's given by a person who turns out to be unkind.

**Cognates:** Cognates, words that look and/or sound similar in two different languages, are a source of support for students learning English. In the context of studying Shakespeare, who himself was a wordsmith, it makes sense for students to familiarize themselves with the etymology, or history, of words, so this idea can work for both English language learners as well as native English speakers students. In this strategy, students record words, alongside the cognate in a second language. Students can ask themselves what words they know in their home language that look or sound like the English word they are analyzing (Cobb & Blachowicz, 2014). Students who are not connecting to a specific second language, can research the etymology of unknown words to determine what cognates might exist in other languages. This strategy benefits students learning Spanish as well as students learning English. The cognates can offer clues to the meaning of their English counterparts. In addition, the discovery of cognates can help students who are developing bilinguals. These examples are in Spanish, though cognates can be found within the text from many different languages.

**Close Read Prompt:** Read the passage to identify unfamiliar words that Shakespeare chose to use. Pay special attention to words that sound like words in Spanish, then research the etymology of the word and explain how its meaning is related in both English and Spanish.

## Examples of Cognates from Act 1 Scene 1
*A Midsummer Night's Dream*

Vexation = *vejacion*
Consent = *consentir*
Impression = *impresion*
Fantasy = *fantasia*
Obedience = *obediencia*
Privilege = *privilegio*

## Romeo and Juliet

Dignity = *dignidad*
Civil = *civil*
Fatal = *fatal*
Continuance = *continuación*

## Hamlet

Figure = *figuridad*
Scholar = *escolar*
Eternity = *eternidad*
Majesty = *majestad*
Offend = *ofender*

### Activity 2: Word Sorts

Word sorts encourage students to make conceptual connections among words and are an effective vocabulary and concept development strategy (Baumann & Kame'enui, 2004; Bear, Invernizzi, Templeton, & Johnston, 2007). Students are given a set of vocabulary word cards. Within groups or partnerships students are faced with the task of grouping their given cards into categories. Categories are determined by the students. This activity can be repeated with different sets of word cards, or by parameters set by the teacher for each of the categories. Such parameters might require that categories be related to characters or theme.

**Time:** One class session to sort, plus time to share.
**Materials:**

- A collection of notecards labeled with words from the text. A set of 15–25 words per team is ideal. Each team can have the same set of words which makes the discussion livelier as teams compare and contrast their groupings.
- Large chart paper to display groupings.

**Steps:**

1. Students are organized into teams of two or three. Each team is given a set of labeled vocabulary cards.
2. Within their groups students must decide how to categorize the words. They may have as many categories as they like so long as each category has at least two words in it. Each word should be categorized.
3. As students discuss and make categorization decisions, circulate and ask questions that require students to explain their thinking. Such questions might include:
    a. I see that you have put _____ and _____ in the same category. What thinking led you to that decision?
    b. Can you explain the relationship between these words?
    c. What possible connections do these two groups of words have?
4. When sharing, students should be able to explain their rationale for categorizing their words. This is a great opportunity to reinforce the skill of making a claim and supporting it with evidence that is required when forming a response to text dependent questions as discussed in Chapter 3.

## Activity 3: The English Language Tree

This activity allows students to see that the English language is a product of many other languages intermingling over time (Burrows, 2022). It involves creating a giant paper tree that represents English. As students discover how many words come from different languages they add and label the branches accordingly. The main fork of the tree is labeled Greek and Latin. Students design and assemble flowers to add to the tree. Each flower contains an English word derived from another language.

124 ◆ Vocabulary and Word Choice

**FIGURE 5.1** This tree serves as a visual metaphor for how the English language has blossomed from many other languages.

**Time:** This activity requires one 50-minute class period, but I also recommend allowing this to be an ongoing opportunity throughout the unit of study. It is a perfect answer to the eternal question: What can I do when I'm done? Add more leaves and flowers to the English Language Tree!

**Materials:**

- Tree trunk with branches fashioned from brown paper.
- Assorted colored paper for creating flowers.

**Steps:**

1. Create a large tree trunk that branches out in two directions like a Y. Create additional branches out of brown paper. You

Vocabulary and Word Choice ◆ 125

will need to make three medium branches and about 10 small branches depending on the number of languages culturally relevant to the students in your class.
2. With students label the trunk "The English Language" and make the point that English is like a tree in that it is a whole language, but it is made up of many different languages or branches.
3. Give an example by labeling each branch of the Y Greek and Latin. Then give an example of an English word that is based on a Greek or Latin Root.
4. Next, add another large branch called Romance languages. Explain to students that the Romance languages (Spanish, Italian, and French) have lent the English language many words. To the Romance language branch add smaller branches labeled Spanish, French, and Italian. As you do, give an example of each using the chart for support.
5. Add another large branch called other languages. To this add smaller branches labeled with the languages that are culturally relevant to your students. For instance, if you have Russian, Hindi, and Arabic-speaking students, add a small branch with each of those languages. Explain to students that English borrows from almost all languages. As you do this, give an example of each. Simply googling "English words that come from (add the language desired)" will deliver many examples.
6. Finally, add the last branch and label it "Words from Shakespeare." Explain to students that Shakespeare invented between 1,500 and 3,000 words that we use today. As you do this, give an example of each using the chart for support.
7. Now that the tree is built, students contribute by creating leaves and flowers that feature words, and information about those words. When the flower is created, students should attach them to the correct branch of the tree.

## Tree of English Word Examples
### Greek

- *Chrono* = time as in chronological.
- *Geo* = Earth as in geography.

## Latin

- *Circ* = round as in circle.
- *Audi* = hear as in audition or audible.

## French

- Energy comes from the Middle French word *énergie*.
- Hotel, menu, and neutral are all French words.

## Spanish

- Barbeque comes from the word *barbacoa*.
- Cargo comes from the verb *cargar* meaning 2to load."
- Savvy comes from the word *sabe* which means "knows."

## Italian

- Solo comes from the Italian word which means alone.
- Money comes from the word *moneta*.
- Quarantine from the word *quarantena*.

## Arabic

- Syrup comes from the word *sharab*.
- Sugar comes from the word *sukkar*.

## Shakespearean

- Horrid.
- Lonely.
- Moonbeam.
- Zany.
- Plus many more.

### Activity 4: Invented Words Dictionary

While the exact number of original words invented is debated, Shakespeare scholars agree that Shakespeare did invent, or was the first to record in writing, nearly 1,700 words of the English language (Bryson, 2007). Beginning with the idea that Shakespeare is responsible for creating words that we use today, this project allows students to develop their knowledge of Greek and Latin roots by combining those roots and other word parts to create words that are made up, but have a definition related to the root they contain. In creating their own word dictionaries students emmulate the creativity of the Bard.

**Time:** This is a project that can be done individually or in small groups. If projects are assigned individually the allotted time should be three to four class sessions. Done in groups, the allotted time is about half of that. Be aware that students may request additional time in class to perfect their projects.

**FIGURE 5.2** A student creates their invented word dictionary while rehersals occur behind them.

Note: In this chapter, an engraving of Shakespeare's face by Charles Droeshout (1623) has been used to protect children's identities in photographs.

**Materials:**

- Student Dictionary Think Sheet.
- Tools for creating a book either digitally or with paper and art items.
- A resource for researching Greek and Latin roots.

**Steps:**

1. Remind students from the introductory lessons that Shakespeare is thought to be responsible for creating hundreds and some think even thousands of words that we regularly use today. Explain that their job is to be wordsmiths like Shakespeare.
2. Your job is to create a dictionary of new words. Each word must contain one root and its meaning must be related to the meaning of the root that it contains. For instance, "ped" means "foot," so I might create a word such as "pedbot" which is a noun that means, "a robot controlled foot that is placed on pets' feet to keep them from running away."
3. First, each student or team will create a poster for three to five roots. The job of the poster is to teach the root to your classmates and serve as part of a reference of Greek and Latin roots. Each poster must contain the root, the meaning of the root, an illustration to help remember the meaning of the root, and three examples of words that contain the root as well as the meaning of those words. Students may use the word web map available at the end of this chapter. These posters will be used as a resource by the entire class for the next steps of the project.
4. Students will create at least ten entries that center on a common theme. For instance, a popular idea when studying *A Midsummer Night's Dream* is to make a dictionary of different types of fairies. When studying *Romeo and Juliet* students have made a dictionary of Friar Lawrence's potions. An idea for *Hamlet* would be a dictionary of different ghosts haunting Elsinore.

5. Each entry should include the word, part of speech, variations, definitions for the word and its variation, a sentence using the word, and an illustration or photograph with a caption that helps us understand what the word means.
6. Finally, the dictionary should include an introduction that explains the unifying theme as well as a cover.
7. Students should be aware that they will be responsible for knowing what each of their roots mean and they will be expected to give examples of how the root is used in existing English language words. A simple assessment listing the root and asking students to provide the meaning and an example word can serve as the measure of student learning.

## Activity 5: Botanicals in Figurative Language

Shakespeare uses many botanical elements throughout his work. Students can explore the botanicals of their heritage and edit the script to include those references. An example might be students of Mexican heritage researching the Sonoran desert. They would discover the poisonous Sonoran Desert toad, and realize that the toad's venom could be used in place of Friar Lawrence's potion. Other examples of botanicals that may be replaced are listed below.

## Examples of Botanicals Used in Figurative Language
### *A Midsummer Night's Dream*

The entire place is set in a botanical wonderland that could lend itself to any setting. In addition, there are magical flowers which could also help to convey an updated setting

### *Romeo and Juliet*

Friar Lawrence deals with a variety of plants, one of which yields the potion that allows Juliet to look like she has died without actually dying. The poison provided by the apothecary Romeo visits to obtain the poison he uses to kill himself in Juliet's tomb provides another opportunity to substitute a botanical more closely related to a new setting.

## Hamlet

Poison used in the duel could come from a plant or animal native to the geographical areas corresponding to student's culture. In addition, the flowers Ophelia is surrounded by in her death can be replaced with flowers appropriate to the student selected setting.

### Activity 6: Translating the Bard

This idea was inspired by the work of Kathy Escamilla through her cross language strategy called *Asi se Dice* ("That's How you Say It!"). According to Escamilla, the strategy was developed, "to validate translation as a constructive and worthwhile endeavor that engages students in a complex sophisticated scrutiny of language and emphasizes the subtleties and nuances of communicating messages across languages" (2014). This is such an elegant strategy to use because it serves multilingual learners while also relating to the unit's essential question: What is the power of language? *Asi se Dice* underscores the idea that language changes over time as students will see that whether translated into modern Spanish or English or any other language there is a difference in how we speak now as compared to then, or in this case, Shakespeare's time.

The difference between simply asking students to translate the text into modern language, or their home language and the *Asi se Dice* strategy is that students decide between making literal or conceptual translations while discussing and evaluating translation options. As they discuss students begin to recognize the complexities of language and how subtly different word combinations and translations convey different meanings. For instance, in the prologue to Act 1 of *Romeo and Juliet* there are several word choices that lead to debate when being translated to more contemporary English, or to student-speak, or to another language entirely. The text reads: "Two households, both alike in dignity in fair Verona where we lay our scene." The words alike, "dignity" and "fair" are ones that students struggle to come to consensus over.

Consider the word fair. If students are doing a translation of the prologue into more contemporary English, they need to consider whether Shakespeare is talking about fair in the sense of beautiful, or fair in the sense of just and equal, and make their word choice for their translation accordingly. Students translating into a home language such as Spanish would need to consider more than 10 different possible translations of the word fair including *razonable, equitativo, justa, hermoso,* and *bueno*. Great conversations come from the struggle to decide which word is the best choice for a translation because conceptual translations are far more subjective. This leads to debate as students grapple with choosing the translation that works best, and it is these evaluative conversations that lead to sustained vocabulary development.

This strategy works best with short, rich text selections. Suggestions for passage translations are provided.

**Time:** This is a project that can be done whole class or within small groups. Depending on the comfort level of students, this can be done in one day, or across several days. My suggestion would be to do this across several days to allow ample discussion time. I might assign four lines to be translated at a time before discussing.

**Materials:**

- Critical Thinking: Translating the Bard.

## Critical Thinking: Translating Shakespeare

Scholar's Name _____

Purpose of Reading: The purpose of this reading is to translate Shakespeare's words into contemporary English or another language in order to increase and strengthen our personal vocabulary.

| Translation 1 | Romeo and Juliet<br>Act 1<br>Prologue | Translation 2 |
|---|---|---|
| | Two households, both alike in dignity, | |
| | In fair Verona, where we lay our scene, | |
| | From ancient grudge break to new mutiny, | |
| | Where civil blood makes civil hands unclean. | |
| | From forth the fatal loins of these two foes | |
| | A pair of star-cross'd lovers take their life; | |
| | Whose misadventured piteous overthrows | |
| | Do with their death bury their parents' strife. | |
| | The fearful passage of their death-mark'd love, | |
| | And the continuance of their parents' rage, | |
| | Which, but their children's end, nought could remove, | |
| | Is now the two hours' traffic of our stage; | |
| | The which if you with patient ears attend, | |
| | What here shall miss, our toil shall strive to mend | |

Copyright material from Jennifer Szwaya (2024), *Shakespeare Amazes in the Classroom*, Routledge

- Passage to translate. This resource is presented with the Prologue from *Romeo and Juliet*; however, this passage can be exchanged for a different passage of the teacher's choosing. Several passages that would work well for this level of analysis are identified by their first lines and are outlined following the steps of the lesson.
- English language dictionary and thesaurus.
- Dictionaries that translate to English from student home languages such as Polish to English or Spanish to English dictionaries or online resources.

**Steps:**

1. Place students into groups of three or four. Students speaking the same home language should be grouped together as they will be translating from English to their home language. Students translating to contemporary English from Shakespeare's English can be grouped together.
2. Teams should record their thinking on the thinking sheet. For each line they should record two different options for translating. Students may use provided resources or their own personal lexicons to come to conclusions.
3. Once the teams decide on two acceptable translations for each of the day's assigned lines, then the teams can either jigsaw to share a wider range of translations, or share out with the group as a whole.
4. Original teams finally reconvene to discuss feedback before marking final translation selections on their thinking sheet.

### *A Midsummer Night's Dream*
### Act 1

- Egeus: "Full of vexation come I with complaint"
- Helena: "Call you me fair? That fair again unsay"
- Helena: "How happy some o'er other some can be!"

## Act 2

- Fairy: "Over hill, over dale"
- Puck: "Thou speak'st aright"
- The argument between Demetrius and Helena
- Oberon: "Pray thee give it me"

## Act 3

- Helena: "Oh spite! Oh hell!"

## Act 4

- Bottom: "I have had a most rare vision"

## Act 5

- Theseus: "More strange than true: I never may believe"

### Romeo and Juliet

## Act 1

- Prologue: "Two households, both alike in dignity"
- Prince: "Rebellious subjects, enemies to peace"
- Benvolio: "Madam, an hour before the worshipped sun"
- Benvolio and Romeo's conversation that begins "Good-morrow, cousin"
- Juliet: "I'll look to like, if looking liking move"
- Mercutio: "O, then, I see Queen Mab hath been with you"

## Act 2

- Romeo: "O, she doth teach the torches to burn bright…"
- Romeo: "But, soft! What light through yonder window breaks?"
- Juliet: "Tis but thy name that is my enemy"

## Act 4

- Friar Lawrence: "Hold, then; go home, be merry, give consent"

## *Hamlet*
### Act 1

- Hamlet: "How weary, stale, flat, and unprofitable"
- Hamlet: "Seems, madam! Nay it is; I know not 'seems'"
- Horatio: "Two nights together had these gentlemen"
- Laertes: "For Hamlet and the trifling of his favour"
- Laertes: "Think it no more… Perhaps he loves you now"
- Ophelia: "I shall the effect of this good lesson keep"
- Polonius: "Yet here, Laertes!"

### Act 2

- Hamlet: "Ay sir; to be honest, as this world goes…"
- Polonius: "Though this be madness, yet there is method in't"
- Hamlet: "Now I am alone. Oh what a rogue and peasant slave am I!"

### Act 3

- Hamlet: "To be or not to be"

## Activity 6: Is That Your Sandwich?

There is an abundance of one sentence lessons on the Web that teach emphasis, but my favorite is called "Is that your sandwich?" The lesson originally appeared on *The Folger Shakespeare* website ages ago, but it is no longer there. This learning experience is inspired by that resource. Students examine how which word one emphasizes, changes the meaning of a sentence, and then apply that learning to their lines and performances.

**Time:** One class session.
**Materials:**

- Scripts.
- Highlighters.

**Steps:**

1. It is most beneficial if students know which parts they will be performing at this point so that they can apply their learning to their performances.

2. Display the sentence, "Is that your sandwich?" Read this sentence aloud. Ask the students what it means.
3. Underline the word "that." Reread the sentence with special emphasis on the word "that." "Is *that* your sandwich?" Ask the students if this sentence has the same meaning, or if it has changed. Then ask how it is different. When we emphasize *that* it is as if the sentence is now asking, Is that thing over there, that does not even really seem to be a sandwich, a sandwich, and does it belong to you?
4. Rewrite the sentence. This time underline the word *your*. Ask the students if this sentence has the same meaning, or if it has changed. Then ask how it is different. When we emphasize the word your it is as if we do not believe that the sandwich could belong to you. With the emphasis of your we are now implying an accusation. Does that sandwich even belong to you, or is it someone else's?
5. Rewrite the sentence a final time, and underline the word *sandwich*. Discuss this new meaning. With the emphasis of the word sandwich is a disbelief that the sandwich is really a sandwich. Is that thing over there actually a sandwich?
6. Debrief by discussing what was newly learned. This may be a great time to refer to the essential question board and add new learning to the question.
7. Finally, have students delve into their scripts and read through their lines to determine which words they plan to emphasize and how their choice of words to emphasize changes the meaning of what their character may be saying.
8. A written component to this lesson might ask students to select a line of theirs, and explain how emphasizing one word of the line as compared to another changes the meaning of what they are saying.

### Activity 7: Visualizing and Interpreting Figurative Language

An interesting close read involves comparing a selection of Shakespeare's text to how it is depicted in film. Such work leads to a discussion about the film maker's interpretation and artistic choices. A follow up activity might require students to then select their own beautiful language example and show how they might depict it for stage or screen.

For example, consider Oberon's words in Act as he describes where fairy queen Titania rests. The imagery within the first few lines is stunning:

> I know a bank where the wild thyme blows,
> Where oxlips and the nodding violet grows,
> Quite over-canopied with luscious woodbine,
> With sweet musk roses and with eglantine.

The lines, as explained by Ken Ludwig in his book *How to Teach Your Children Shakespeare*, first must be deciphered by considering individual vocabulary words. First, wild thyme blowing refers to the fragrant herb in bloom. Imagine that. The warm fragrance of thyme in full bloom across the bank wafting across the grass. Oxlips, woodbine, violet, musk roses, and eglantine can be Googled to discover that they are all flowers. Consider the description of the violets nodding. Are they nodding with sleepiness, or are they nodding, as in bowing down to a special person – such as a fairy queen? Working to untangle the meaning of "over canopied" leads us to imagine all of these blooming plants and flowers arching over this special space. The fact that the woodbine is luscious gives the impression of flowers in their most full blossom. Finally eglantine evokes elegance – also suited to our fairy queen. After discussing the text with students and making meaning by deciphering vocabulary with reason, dictionaries, and Google images students can be driven to the conclusion that this is a most beautiful space.

Students now have an understanding of the text which will allow them to be critics of how Oberon's description is portrayed on film. Because the students have a clear sense of what the author is describing they can now evaluate the filmmaker's choices. To further deepen student's evaluation process have them create an illustration of the text, or a plan for how they would go about recreating the Bard's words for the screen. This way, students can also compare the film maker's interpretation to their own. The following questions can facilitate a discussion that evaluates how well a film maker portrayed Shakespeare's words for the screen. While any text selection deemed visually meaningful for the reader can be used for this activity, recommended passages are provided.

## Passages
### A Midsummer Night's Dream

- Act 2 Scene 1, the fairy begins, "Over Hill over dale"
- Act 2 Scene 1, Oberon begins, "I know a bank where the wild thyme blows"
- Act 3 Scene 1, Titania begins, "Be kind and courteous to this gentleman"

### Romeo and Juliet

- Act 1 Prologue, begins, "Two households"
- Act 1 Scene 4, Mercutio begins, "O, Then, I see Queen Mab hath been with you"
- Act 2 Scenes 1 and 2, Romeo begins, "But soft! What light through yonder window breaks?"

### Hamlet

- Act 1 Scene 3, Polonius begins, "Yet here, Laertes!"
- Act 3 Scene 1, Hamlet begins, "To be, or not to be"
- Act 4 Scene 7, Gertrude begins, "There is a willow grows aslant a brook"

## Considerations

In an article titled *Rethinking Vocabulary Instruction* (2004), Professor Karen Bromley reminds educators of the importance of enthusiasm. She argues that to implement sound vocabulary instruction, enthusiasm is number one of nine best practices. "When you appreciate out-of-the-ordinary, powerful, and appealing word use with students and engage them in word play, you share your interest and enjoyment." This is a kind of word consciousness is a successful aspect of vocabulary programs

(Graves & Watts-Taffe, 2002). Being enthusiastic about vocabulary can inspire students to love words and excel in their vocabulary studies.

## Revisiting Essential Unit Question

What is the power of language?

As students work on vocabulary activities, it is important to draw their attention to the overall essential question so that the idea web can grow. During your work on vocabulary, students will see these connections with your help: Language is a way to communicate our feelings, words have meaning – but our emphasis on certain words can really change the meaning, words can put us into different places, words can help us express complicated feelings, words can help us avoid conflicts, and so on. The following questions can help prompt discussions that will lead to new discoveries being added to the Web.

> During your work on vocabulary, students will see these connections with your help: Language is a way to communicate our feelings, words have meaning – but our emphasis on certain words can really change the meaning, words can put us into different places, words can help us express complicated feelings, words can help us avoid conflicts, and so on.

- Let's pretend you are in an argument with your friend or your mom. How can choosing to emphasize of deemphasize certain words help or hinder the situation?
- How would we communicate without language?
- How can language help us avoid conflict?
- How does being able to express our feelings and thoughts improve society?

## References

Baumann, J., & Kame'enui, E. (Eds.). (2004). *Vocabulary instruction: Research to practice*. Guilford Press.

Bear, D., Invernizzi, M., Templeton, S., & Johnston, F. (2007). *Words their way: Word study for phonics, vocabulary, and spelling instruction* (4th ed.). Prentice Hall.

Bryson, B. (2007). *Shakespeare: The world as a stage*. Atlas Books/HarperPress.

Bromley, K. (2007). Nine things every teacher should know about words and vocabulary instruction. *Journal of Adolescent & Adult Literacy, 50*(7), 528–537.

Burrows, H. (2022). *The influence of other languages on English: Cambridge English*. https://www.cambridge.org/elt/blog/2021/06/22/the-influence-other-languages-english/

Cobb, C., & Blachowicz, C. (2014). *No more "look up the list" vocabulary instruction*. Heinemann.

Escamilla, K. (2014). *Biliteracy from the start: Literacy squared in action*. Caslon Publishing.

Graves, M. F., & Watts-Taffe, S. M. (2002). The place of word consciousness in a research-based vocabulary program. *What Research Has to Say About Reading Instruction*, 140–165. https://doi.org/10.1598/0872071774.7

Harper, L. (2016, February 20). *Strategies for effective vocabulary instruction*. https://www.academia.edu/22218181/STRATEGIES_FOR_EFFECTIVE_VOCABULARY_INSTRUCTION

Lamb, C. & Lamb, M. (1807). *Tales from Shakespeare*. Juvenile Library of William Godwin.

Lawrence, J. (2009). Summer reading: Predicting adolescent word learning from aptitude, time spent reading, and text type. *Reading Psychology, 30*(5), 445–465.

Ludwig, K. (2013). *How to teach your children shakespeare*. Crown.

McKeown, M., Beck, I., Omanson, R., & Pople, M. (1985). Some effects of the nature and frequency of vocabulary instruction on the knowledge and use of words. *Reading Research Quarterly, 20*(5), 522–535.

Nagy, W., Herman, P., & Anderson, R. C. (1985). Learning words from context. *Reading Research Quarterly, 20*(2), 233–253.

National Governors Association Center for Best Practices & Council of Chief State School Officers. (2010). *Common core state standards for English language arts and literacy in history/social studies, science, and technical subjects*.

Serravallo, J. (2015). *Reading strategies book*. Heinemann Educational Books.

Shakespeare, W. (1596). *A midsummer night's dream*.

Shakespeare, W. (1597). *Romeo and Juliet*.

Shakespeare, W. (1601). *Hamlet*.

# 6
# Point of View

Doubting Diannah was not having any of Romeo on the day she met him. Her fifth-grade self was not impressed. She would soon confront him with a giant remote control that was being exquisitely crafted by our set designers for that year's performance of *Romeo and Juliet*. Because of Doubting Diannah our audience would be getting an unfamiliar take on *Romeo and Juliet*. In our production, Diannah would have the power to pause the action to deliver her incredulous takes on Romeo and Juliet's choices.

"Romeo is ridiculous. There is NO way he really loves Juliet. He, like juuuust had the hots for Rosaline. And now he wants to MARRY HER? What!!!!????" Her criticisms only escalated after the final scene – "Now they're both dead? This is INSANE! This cannot be how this ends." Eventually, her exasperation became a judgment on our plans to perform in front of their gifted colleagues in the lower grades – "We cannot share this ending with third graders!" Because of Diannah's point of view on the plot, which was informed through our study of characters' points of view within the text, our audience saw a version of *Romeo and Juliet* with an entirely new ending. In Diannah's class's version, Romeo and Juliet make different choices and, as a result, end up skipping off

> "Romeo is ridiculous. There is NO way he really loves Juliet. He, like juuuust had the hots for Rosaline. And now he wants to MARRY HER? What!!!!????"

to Mantua with plans to get to know each other better instead of getting married and then "getting dead."

In this chapter, students explore character motivation and point of view through several of the most prescient questions facing adolescents: How much control should parents have on life decisions made by young adults? What is needed to form a strong friendship, including with boyfriends or girlfriends? To what extent do revenge and violence effectively resolve conflicts? This module of the unit requires students to investigate characters' motivations and points of view as it pertains to our thematic questions. To do so, students take on the persona of one of the studied characters and engage in a debate. Often, students want to make adaptations to the story at this point, add a character to change the ending of the story, or add a monologue in which a character reflects and makes a plot-altering decision.

## Instruction: Learning Goals in Reading Literature

The learning goals for this chapter are all related to point of view. Early in the continuum, students work to discern the difference between first- and third-person point of view. As the students progress, their exploration of point of view becomes more nuanced and they strive to determine how a character's point of view influences the description of events. Next, students attempt to explain how an author develops different characters' point of view. Towards the end of the continuum, students begin analyzing how different characters' points of view contrast, until they finally work to consider how differing points of view create effects such as suspense and humor.

Stating learning goals directly will help students identify the purpose of instruction and thus be more likely to achieve it. Specifically, the activities in this module will lead students to understand the similarities and differences in point of view as well as the role point of view plays in developing the humor and suspense of a text. This can be stated as follows for students: "I can determine the point of view and explain how it is developed over the course of a text."

## Module Learning Goals

| | Going Far | | | | |
|---|---|---|---|---|---|
| | 4 | 5 | 6 | 7 | 8 |
| | Distinguish between first- and third-person narration. | Explain how a speaker's point of view influences how events are described. | Explain how an author develops the point of view of the narrator or speaker in a text. | Analyze how an author develops and contrasts the points of view of different characters or narrators in a text. | Analyze how differences in the points of view of the characters and the audience or reader create such effects as suspense or humor. |
| | Going Deep | | | | |
| | I participated in a role play situation, reflected on the various points of view present within the scene, and analyzed the reliability of different characters. | | | | |
| | I completed a spoken, written, or performed piece that considers the inner voice or alter ego of a character. | | | | |
| | I developed and presented an aside that I would like to add to my character's lines. | | | | |

The benchmarks for this learning goal were established using the Common Core Standards.

## Instruction: Assessments

The following prompts increase in complexity and can be used as an assessment tool. Student responses may come in various product forms including a written or spoken response, a student designed and completed graphic organizer, or a digital presentation using the application of choice.

Consider an event in the text. Write a short first-person account of the event from the perspective of a character of your choice. Then write a short third-person account of the same event.

Consider an event in the text. Write a short description of that event from the perspective of two different characters. Then, explain how those descriptions differ and why.

Consider the characters and the problems they face. Explain one character's point of view regarding a specific event or problem. How do you know exactly what that character's perspective is? Use text evidence to explain how the author gives this character a point of view.

Consider the characters and the problems they face. Explain two or more characters' points of view regarding a specific event or problem. How do you know exactly what each character's perspective is? Use text evidence to explain how the author creates contrasting points of view among characters.

Explain an example in which two or more characters' contrasting points of view creates suspense or humor. Provide evidence from the text that supports your reasoning.

## Instruction: Learning Activities

### Activity 1: Point of View Role Play

In this activity, students play roles within scenarios that have conflicts similar to those found in Shakespeare's stories. Through a dramatization of scenarios, students investigate differing perspectives, analyze the point of view of their assigned role, act out the scenario according to those perspectives, and then discuss. The activity can be extended to include role writing, which further deepens students' understanding of perspective.

**Time:** This activity is best done before or during a first reading of the text. The activity takes one to two class sessions, or more, depending on if the writing element is added.

**Materials:**

- Dramatic scenarios

### *A Midsummer Night's Dream*

**Characters:**

A teacher who gives an unfair assignment
A student who is stuck between a rock and a hard place
The student's parent or caregiver

**Scene**: You are a student who has been working on an assignment for a very demanding teacher. Even though you know that the teacher wants what's best for you, you are overwhelmed by the work that needs to get done – especially since you have not spent as much time working on it as you should have done. Now, in class you have just been informed that the due date is closer than you expected. When you speak up, the teacher tells you your only option is to fail the class if you do not get the assignment done in time. You know your family will support the teacher. What should you, the student, do?

## Romeo and Juliet

**Characters**:

A student who comes across a conflict
A second student who is a friend of the first and in a conflict with
    a third student
A third student
A police officer

**Scene**: You are walking down the street when you see your friend arguing with another kid from school. The other kid has threatened you before, but you avoided a fight. As you approach them, you hear your friend defending you. Their argument becomes more physical and you try to discourage a fight, but soon fists are flying and punches are thrown. Your friend gets punched very hard and collapses. You jump in and defend your friend. Your fist makes contact with the other kid from school. Once you hit him he does not get back up. An officer approaches the scene. Who is responsible for the other kid's injury?

## Hamlet

**Characters**:

A teacher who has brought a treat for the class
A principal who is drinking a soda labeled with another teacher's name
A student who sees the principal drinking the soda

**Scene**: You are at school. Your teacher brought a treat for your class that needs to be refrigerated, so they ask you to bring it to the teacher's lunch room and put it in the refrigerator. When you get to the room, there is another adult at the fridge – the principal. As the principal greets you notice they have pulled a can of soda out and are drinking it. On the can you see your teacher's name written in Sharpie. Later that day, as your teacher is passing out the treat, she takes one herself. This surprises you since you never see her eat sweets. When you mention this, your teacher says she decided to splurge on a treat since she didn't have a soda with her lunch. What should you, the student, do?

**Steps:**

1. Organize students into teams of three or four. Distribute a copy of the scenario to each team and instruct students to choose roles. If students are hesitant to perform short dramatizations, teams of four might be considered. In teams of four there might be two students for each role: A playwright and an actor. While all students complete the thinking work for the activity, the playwright documents ideas, and the actors perform them.
2. Direct students to read their scenario. Students should imagine a conversation that would occur between the characters in order to resolve the question posed in the scenario. They might dramatize the conversation at this point.
3. Next, instruct students to analyze their speaker's reliability. Which speaker is more reliable? Why? Consider how the unreliable character may behave.
4. After determining their character's reliability, students should prepare for performing their skits in front of the class. Students should focus on what their character might say given their level of reliability.
5. After performing skits for the class, the group should discuss the following questions:
    a. Which information was stressed by characters? Why do you think this might be?
    b. Which information was left out by characters? Why do you think this might be?

6. Following the debrief, an in-role writing prompt can be used to further examine point of view. After organizing students into groups of four or five, have two students maintain the original roles. Then, have the group decide which two or three additional character perspectives they might like to add. Perhaps a passerby, or a friend, or another authority figure. After students practice having the conversation, have them reflect by writing a journal describing the situation as they saw it within their role compared to how they see the situation as themselves. Students should write for five to ten minutes before sharing within their groups.

## Activity 2: Rewind and Replay

In this activity, students perform sections of the text, and then "rewind the text" to replay it with character commentary. The character commentary takes the form of added asides in which the characters explain how they are thinking and feeling in the situation that was just performed. And, those thoughts and feelings should be spoken by the character's inner voice or alter ego (Smith & Wilhelm, 2010). Alternately, the scene might be performed with a giant pause button, which any character may press in order to stop the action and comment. Groups of students can perform different scenes and replay them with commentary from various characters in the scene, or several scenes that include the same actor can be performed with that one character's commentary shared after the "rewind."

**Time:** Two to three class sessions
**Materials:**

- Something to serve as a pause button – this could be a drawing on the board

**Steps:**

1. Organize students into groups. Each group will need a part of a scene to perform and enough members to perform it. Scenes can be chosen by students if the goal of the lesson is to simply work with the concept of perspective and

perspective-taking. If, however, students are working at a higher level, they might consider characters' perspectives relative to a specific theme.
2. Teams should then close read their text to identify and annotate parts where their character or another character might have a thought, feeling, or insight to share. I recommend having students do this reading aloud to allow students to practice fluency and to facilitate identifying spots in which a character might have more to share than what they are saying. This direction can be given as is, more open ended, or in conjunction with a specific question such as one related to theme. An open ended approach allows students to focus on the idea that different characters have different ideas about what is happening in the story and why. Attaching a specific question related to theme allows students to gather text evidence that will support their thinking as they write about theme.
3. Next, students should annotate the specific thoughts that they think the character might be having. After, teams should share and discuss their individual annotations and come to consensus about when each character should pause the action to comment. Teams should also agree to the gist of what each character's comments will be.
4. Team members take time to revise their part of the script to add their commentary. Enough time should be afforded to this step to allow students to produce well written additions. Since this is a short writing assignment it is perfect to practice peer editing.
5. Next, with updated scripts, students should rehearse before performing for the class. After performing, the class might discuss how the scene changed or added to their thinking about character/theme, etc.

6. To extend this activity students might complete a writing assignment in which they respond to a related text dependent question. Such an activity can also serve as an assessment. Student thinking might be assessed through a product of the student's choosing.

## Activity 3: Perspective Sort

In this activity, students deeply investigate the text to determine different characters' perspectives on various conflicts within the plot. The investigation prepares them to produce a piece of in-role writing that brings a character's personal perspective to life. In-role writing is an exercise that requires students to write from the perspective of a character in the form of a letter, email, text, journal, or other form. Strong in-role writing will include plot predictions based on inferences made about a character's motivations, beliefs, opinions, and feelings.

**Time:** Several class sessions
**Materials:**

- Critical Thinking: Consider Different Perpsectives

## Critical Thinking: Consider Different Perspectives

Scholar's Name: _____

Issue or Problem to Be Analyzed According to Character's Perspective: _____

_____

Character 1's Perspective: _____

| Perspective or Claim<br>What do you think would be the character's point of view on the issue or problem? State it below. | Literal<br>List two pieces of evidence that support what you think the character's point of view is. These are direct quotes from the text. | Inferential<br>Explain what you can infer from the literal evidence, and how you know this. |
|---|---|---|
| | 1.<br><br><br>2. | |

Create one piece of in-role writing that proposes the character's imagined response to the situation:

_____
_____
_____
_____
_____

Copyright material from Jennifer Szwaya (2024), *Shakespeare Amazes in the Classroom*, Routledge

Character 2's Perspective: _____

| **Perspective or Claim** | **Literal** | **Inferential** |
|---|---|---|
| What do you think would be the character's point of view on the issue or problem? State it below. | List two pieces of evidence that support what you think the character's point of view is. These are direct quotes from the text. | Explain what you can infer from the literal evidence, and how you know this. |

1.

2.

Create one piece of in-role writing that proposes the character's imagined response to the situation:

_____
_____
_____
_____
_____

Briefly explain the difference in perspectives between the two characters:

_____
_____
_____

**Steps:**

1. Begin brainstorming a list with students of issues and problems present in the text on which characters may have different perspectives.

## *A Midsummer Night's Dream*

- Marriage of Hermia and Lysander
- Puck's use of the love flower

## *Romeo and Juliet*

- Romeo and his friends sneaking into the Capulets' party
- Conflict that leads to the death of Tybalt and Mercutio

## *Hamlet*

- Hamlet decides to follow the ghost in Act 1
- Ophelia is rejected by Hamlet

2. Explain to students that they will be considering the issues from multiple points of view and providing evidence, both literal and inferential, to support their conclusions about the perspectives of various characters.
3. Students should identify the characters who might have a specific perspective with regards to the scene. For each character involved in the scene, students should record the following information: Two direct quotes from the text that provide insight about how the character feels or thinks about the situation, and one piece of in-role writing that proposes the character's imagined response to the situation. Teams should record their writing on a Critical Thinking: Perspective document.
4. After Critical Thinking: Perspectives are completed, teams or the teacher should record the information in each cell of

the chart on its own notecard. Notecards should be paired up with a blank Critical Thinking: Perspective document that is labeled with the issue or problem.
5. On day two, teams should receive a set of prepared notecards and their corresponding blank chart for an issue or problem that is different from the one they prepared the previous day. The task for the team is to organize the notecards into the chart for this new issue. After teams organize their notecards onto the chart, then the teams should reach out to the notecard creators to check their charts for accuracy.
6. At day three of this activity, students will have analyzed two different scenarios or problems from multiple perspectives. This prepares them with the knowledge necessary to create a detailed piece of writing in which they take on the perspective of one of the characters.

### Activity 4: Alter Ego/Inner Voice

Characters, like people in real life, often think more than they may choose to speak aloud. Smith and Wilhelm (2010) discuss several ideas that support students in their efforts to uncover characters' unspoken thoughts and feelings. In alter-ego writing, sometimes referred to as inner-voice drama, characters share their inner dialogue. These dialogues may reveal characters' more hidden motives, feelings, thoughts, and opinions. This concept can be clarified for students by asking: "What do you think the character is thinking or feeling, but not saying right now?" If students are still struggling with this idea the example of being lectured by a parent is a goldmine. The teacher might say, "think about the last time your parents or guardians were scolding you. It does not matter if you were right or wrong, what matters is what you were thinking as you were bring lectured to. Did you imagine rolling your eyes? Argue back, only in your mind? What were you saying to yourself? This is your alter ego or your inner voice. Now, let's imagine the inner voices of the characters in different situations."

**FIGURE 6.1** A student writes about perspective while classmates fashion costumes out of tulle and drawn flowers.

Note: In this chapter, an engraving of Shakespeare's face by Charles Droeshout (1623) has been used to protect children's identities in photographs.

**Time:** Several class sessions
**Materials:** Selected text passages
**Steps:**

1. Decide whether to have the whole class focus on one character in one situation, multiple characters in one situation, one character in multiple situations, or multiple characters in multiple situations. Experience tells me that focusing on one character in multiple situations is helpful if the intended focus is on analyzing a particular character's development over the course of a text. Focusing on one situation in which multiple characters' perspectives are considered is a good option if the focus is on how characters' points of view affect

how events are described. Another option is to examine how the same two characters see several different situations. This is an excellent option if the desired end result is a compare and contrast piece. First, determine your instructional goal, then choose the scope of student work.
2. Next, select text excerpts for each issue being examined. This is something student teams can do, or the text selections can be identified by the teacher ahead of time. Excerpts might come from a mix of the Lamb stories, the included abridged Shakespearean plays, the complete Shakespearean texts available widely for free, or film clips (see Chapter 8). Students should reread selected excerpts in a close read format in the style of reading two in which they are annotating for specific details. For instance, students in a group of four are examining the scene in which Marcellus and Horatio take Hamlet to meet the ghost. The team has identified all of the texts that relay this scene. Now they should read and annotate the text for words that reveal each of the character's feelings in the moment. Students might choose a different color for each character or each annotate a different character, and then share their findings with the group.
3. Now that the group has analyzed texts relating to a specific issue or situation and annotated for each character's possible thoughts and feelings on the topic students are ready to make inferences about what the characters may be thinking or feeling, but not saying.
4. Students should use their inferences to imagine the internal dialogue the characters are experiencing. Students can share their thinking in multiple ways including:
    a. A skit in which one student plays the character as is, while another plays their alter ego reading the script created by an individual student or the team.
    b. A comic in which a character's thought bubbles are filled with the thinking of the character's alter ego as imagined by the student or group.
    c. Character diary or journal entries.
5. As students finish, they should share with the class in a debrief session in which different imagined alter-ego voices

are evaluated for reasonableness – that is, does the text provide evidence to support the inferences made by students about character's alter egos, and why the character would want to keep certain information, thoughts, or feelings to themselves.

## Activity 5: Debates

Debating questions related to theme within the framework of point of view achieves several things. First, it helps students distinguish their point of view from the character's point of view and from the author's point of view. Second, it prepares students to write about theme by allowing them to investigate a topic from multiple perspectives and gather evidence. Finally, it provides opportunity for students to practice their speaking and listening skills.

**Time:** Several class periods to prepare, and one class period to debate. Additional time may be used for students to reflect on how the debate informed their point of view on the topic.

**Materials:**

- Students will need a debate organizer sheet, and a question to debate
- Students will also need their copies of the text to refer to as they seek evidence as to different characters' perspectives on the topic at hand

**Steps:**

1. If students are not familiar with debate it is helpful to complete some direct instruction regarding debate format and terminology such as claim/point, counterclaim/counterpoint, rebuttal, logos, ethos, and pathos. Watching video clips of debates can be helpful as well. There are a multitude of resources on different debate structures available online, including the parliamentary approach which is the most commonly used at the college level. A variety of debate models can be located through a google search to inform the structure of the debate, if the one proposed here is too simplistic for your students. The format described below is loosely based on the Middle School Debate Program.

2. Establish the claim to be argued. In order to support students' work with theme, I have always selected topics that facilitate student investigation of theme and enable them to prepare to write about theme. Statements that have worked well for each text are listed below, but please keep in mind that the topics that can be debated are not limited to the examples provided below. Let your students' interests drive what is debated.

   *Hamlet*
   Revenge is an effective strategy for dealing with conflict
   To be a good parent one must be honest with their children at all times

   *Romeo and Juliet*
   Young people are capable of making good decisions about their lives and futures
   Violence is an effective strategy for dealing with conflict

   *A Midsummer Night's Dream*
   Good friends are always loyal
   Children should always obey their parents

3. Organize students into two teams. Within the teams, some members should represent characters, who will speak to their own perspective on the topic being debated, while other members will be themselves, offering a student reader's perspective on the topic. In organizing the teams this way, the fact that a text contains the character's perspective while the reader brings their own perspective is highlighted. It also reinforces the idea that there are several different points of view present when a text is being read. One team should be the proposition team. This is the team that agrees with the statement being debated. The other team is the opposition team and they are responsible for arguing that the claim is false.
4. Teams should work together to identify points that their team would like to make. Students debating as characters should find evidence from the text that they would bring up in character to support or refute the claim being argued. Students debating as themselves should work to find supporting

evidence for their points from resources outside of the text such as newspaper articles, library books, and other resources that provide supporting evidence and/or data. Student and in-character debaters can also support each other's work. Each team will need a first speaker, a second speaker, and a rebuttal speaker. If teams have more than three members, additional speakers or rebuttal speakers can be added. The debate seems to work best when students debating as characters from the text are the speakers, and students speaking as students offer rebuttals; however, it is not absolutely necessary to organize the debate in this manner.
5. Teams should prepare their points by completing the debate organizer. Teams should also rehearse making their points and rebuttals.
6. The format of the debate and timing is as follows. More speaker and or rebuttals can be added as needed depending on the number of students participating. During their speeches, the proposition and opposition each have —two to three minutes to make a point, which receives a —one- or two-minute counterpoint during the rebuttal. A variation on the structure that makes the debate more lively is to complete a rebuttal after each of the opposition and propositions points.
Proposition team: Speaker 1 – 2–3 minutes
Opposition team: Speaker 1 – 2–3 minutes
Proposition team: Speaker 2 – 2–3 minutes
Opposition team: Speaker 2 – 2–3 minutes
Proposition team: Rebuttal Speaker 1 – 1–2 minutes
Opposition team: Rebuttal Speaker 2 – 1–2 minutes
7. To make the debate more exciting and interactive, parliamentary debate rules of heckling and disagreeing may be included. To disagree with a point being made, participants may call out the word, "Shame!" And to agree, participants may gently pound or tap their tabletops.
8. The debate activity can end with a guest judge weighing in on which side offered more sound arguments and rebuttals and offering feedback. In addition, students can complete a piece of reflective writing on the topic being debated to solidify their own point of view on the topic.

## Activity 6: Reliability Sort

One important consideration a reader has when considering point of view is reliability. How well can the character who is telling the story be trusted? And to what degree is what they tell the audience or reader impacted by their own feelings about a situation? For instance, in Act 1 Scene 1 of *Hamlet*, Claudius basically tells Hamlet to stop being sad about his father's death because after all, all fathers die at some point. Is Claudius' advice trustworthy, or does it serve Claudius' own interests if Hamlet just moves on and gets over the loss of his father? Are we hearing the full version of events or are key details being left out? In the case of Claudius giving Hamlet advice about grief, it is difficult to say that Claudius is being altruistic because if Hamlet follows the advice Claudius is giving then it works out very well for Claudius. If Hamlet simply accepts his father's death then he will not be asking questions and digging around to find the truth. It is in Claudius' best interests for Hamlet to stop hunting for the truth, thus when he gives Hamlet advice, it is not to be trusted. Reliability drives students to ask whether or not a narrator or character is trustworthy or perhaps motivated to be dishonest. In the following activity, students develop a checklist for determining whether or not a narrator is reliable, and then apply the checklist and gather text evidence to support their thinking.

**Time:** One to two class periods
**Materials:**

- Chart paper
- Little heads of each of the characters – students might create these

**Steps:**

1. Begin the lesson with a T chart projected or written on chart paper. One side of the T should read: "Reliable and Trustworthy," while the other should read: "Unreliable and Not Trustworthy." Create a nested T chart on each side of the larger T chart. The nested chart for each side should read: "Character" on one side and "Behaviors" on the other.

2. Discuss with students the idea of reliability and trustworthiness. Include and ask for examples of people in life who are more or less reliable and ask students what they think makes such people either reliable or unreliable. Then explain that groups will be discussing characters from the text and determining their reliability or lack of reliability.
3. Sort students into groups. Distribute character faces to groups if they were prepared ahead of time, or have students create a little head for their character. Have students discuss the character and come to consensus about where the character should be placed – on the reliable or unreliable side. Then, have students collect two to three examples from the text that support their thinking.
4. As teams finish, groups present their findings, and record their information on the class chart.

## Activity 7: Asides

Throughout *Romeo and Juliet*, *Hamlet*, and *A Midsummer Night's Dream*, Shakespeare employs asides in his writing. Asides are a bit of theater magic that indicate a character's lines are being spoken to the audience alone, and that the rest of the characters cannot hear what is being said. The effect often creates a humorous moment between the actor and the audience and provides the audience with information or insights that the rest of the characters are not privy to. Because asides offer an unfiltered glimpse of a character's point of view they are an excellent text resource when attempting to discern a character's perspective.

**Time:** One to two class periods
**Materials:**

- Copy of shortened Shakespeare text

**Steps:**

1. Students should be made aware of the purpose of reading. In this case, it is to identify uses of an aside and to analyze the aside to determine the character's point of view. Individually or in teams, students can scan the text to locate asides, or a list of asides to be studied can be provided by the teacher.

*Hamlet*
Hamlet in Act 1 Scene 2
Lord Polonius in Act 2 Scene 2

*Romeo and Juliet*
Romeo has an aside in Act 2 Scenes 1 and 2
Friar Lawrence in Act 4 Scene 1

*A Midsummer Night's Dream*
Puck has three asides in Act 3 Scene 1

2. Once asides are identified, individually, or within partnerships or larger teams, students should complete a close reading of the aside assigned to their group.
   What is happening in the scene?
   What is the character telling the audience in the aside?
   What does the aside tell us about the character's point of view?
   Why wouldn't they want the other characters to hear?
   What information did the aside give the audience or reader that the other characters do not know?
   What do you think Shakespeare intended the effect of the aside to be on the audience?
3. Students can share their thinking in a group discussion or in writing.
4. An interesting extension of this activity would be to have students write an additional aside for a character in a scene to capture their point of view, or to bring humor to the scene. For instance, if Ophelia were to give an aside when would it be? And in what situation? I can imagine she might have some thoughts to share with the audience about Hamlet's behavior during the play he has performed in front of Claudius and Gertrude! Similarly, the Nurse might have some comments about Romeo to share with the audience when in Act 3 Scene 3 she finds him immaturely throwing a near temper tantrum at Friar Lawrence's after he has been banished from Verona.

## Considerations

Students who speak a language other than English at home often find it easiest to express intense feelings, emotions, and ideas in their native language. This fact can be accommodated through having any inner-voice dialogue or asides added into the script in the student's native language. This would make the character that they play bilingual which is another way that students can adapt Shakespeare's work to make it a better reflection of who the students are.

## Revisiting Essential Unit Question

### What Is the Power of Language?

Within this study of point of view students may gather several new insights about the power of language. One, they see that through debate language allows us to explore and resolve conflicts together as it gives us a system for explaining our thoughts and feelings about an issue or topic. Students can also be led to see that our point of view is part of our identity, so language is another way for us to express our identity.

> Students can also be led to see that our point of view is part of our identity, so language is another way for us to express our identity.

## References

Lamb, C., & Lamb, M. (1807). *Tales from Shakespeare*. Juvenile Library of William Godwin.

*Middle school public debate program*. (n.d.). https://www.esuus.org/esu/programs/middle_school_debate/educators/quote_2/MSPDP_V4_Teachers_Guide_2_Small:en-us.pdf

National Governors Association Center for Best Practices & Council of Chief State School Officers. (2010). *Common core state standards for English language arts and literacy in history/social studies, science, and technical subjects*.

Shakespeare, W. (1596). *A midsummer night's dream*.

Shakespeare, W. (1597). *Romeo and Juliet*.
Shakespeare, W. (1601). *Hamlet*.
Smith, M. W., & Wilhelm, J. D. (2010). *Fresh takes on teaching literary elements: How to teach what really matters about character, setting, point of view and theme*. Scholastic.

# 7
# Multimedia

One of the most perplexing moments in my teaching career arrived when I was educated by my students about the phenomena that is "unboxing" videos on YouTube. Unboxing videos feature people opening new items, sometimes gift wrapped, for their audience. Slowly but enthusiastically a range of hosts build anticipation while revealing the contents. For the life of me, I could not understand why this was so completely engaging for the kids. It reminded me of the jealousy I felt watching kids open their birthday gifts at parties I had attended as a child. Regardless, my students were big fans, until I ruined it for them by introducing the question of motivation. Why would people do this? Why do they want *you* as their audience? Is the host manipulating your feelings? How? And, finally, why? Who does showing kids unboxing videos help? After considering that the toy makers might be paying the unboxing stars to motivate kids to want to buy toys by making them feel excited and envious, the kids were outraged, but ultimately still big fans of the genre. I still take it as a win though, because I know that they are at least aware of the fact that multimedia content has ulterior motives. This is a small but important first step to being media literate.

We need to teach kids how to be critical about the media that enters their brain – to be critical consumers. Consider how much content comes through to kids through video and images. Given the fact that kids ages eight to 12 spend an average of four to nearly eight hours a day in front of screens, we know it must be

DOI: 10.4324/9781003361107-7

a ton (AACAP, n.d.; Generation M2, 2010). We must teach students how to view media critically. A first step is in considering the media content creators and their perspective, intent, needs, and reasons for reaching an audience. How do we decipher the implicit messages conveyed in media? While watching clips of Shakespeare's text interpreted through the media of film, music, and art will not make children impervious to media manipulation, it will facilitate the process as students learn how be viewers with a critical eye to the impact of camera angles, music, lighting, color, etc., on how they feel and respond to the media.

Aside from the important goal of developing media-savvy students, incorporating media into the study of Shakespeare is helpful because seeing the text performed can improve comprehension, especially when a scene depicting complex plot points is viewed and analyzed. Further, the film clips can work as a secondary text to gather supporting evidence when making a claim.

> Aside from the important goal of developing media savvy students, incorporating media into the study of Shakespeare is helpful because seeing the text performed can improve comprehension, especially when a scene depicting complex plot points is viewed and analyzed.

Beware! When showing films based on Shakespeare one must be prepared for codpieces and cigarettes. It's not an easy choice when planning for an audience of seventh graders. Either way the jeers, and *oooohs*, and giggles will make an appearance. Be prepared. For this reason I advise against simply sitting the students in front of any of the films described in this chapter. From the BBC's *Animated Tales of Shakespeare* to Baz Luhrmann's 1996 modernization of *Romeo and Juliet* and beyond there is content that may cause a ruckus in nearly every compelling film version of *Hamlet*, *Romeo and Juliet*, and *A Midsummer Night's Dream*. For this reason, I strongly advise that you review each clip or resource yourself ahead of time. Although I have never had a negative experience as a result of showing media content related to Shakespeare, resources described in this chapter may not be a good fit for your current class. I also recommend checking with your students' families. Sending home a detailed explanation of the exact scenes you will be showing, what they contain, the purpose for showing, and how the students will benefit from viewing can generate trust and avoid conflict.

## Learning Goals

In working with multimedia related learning goals, students begin by making connections between the text and media by identifying places in which the media mirrors the text. Next, students focus on how the media contributes to the meaning, tone, and beauty of the text. At the following level, students reflect on the experience of reading the text and experiencing the multimedia by comparing and contrasting the two. At the most complex stage, students compare and contrast a text to its multimedia version while analyzing the effects of different techniques such as camera angles, before finally considering how a multimedia version of a text varies from or remains true to the original text.

Stating learning goals directly will help students identify the purpose of instruction and thus be more likely to achieve it. Learning goals related to multimedia can be phrased as follows for students: I can make connections, analyze, and compare and contrast the text with multimedia versions of the text.

**Module Rubric**

| Going Far | | | | |
|---|---|---|---|---|
| 4 | 5 | 6 | 7 | 8 |
| Make connections between the text and a visual or oral presentation. Identify where each version reflects specific descriptions and directions in the text. | Analyze how visual and multimedia elements contribute to the meaning, tone, or beauty of a text. | Compare and contrast the experience of reading a text to listening or viewing an audio video or live version of the text. | Compare and contrast a text to its multimedia version analyzing the effects of techniques. | Analyze how a multimedia version of a text remains true or departs from an original text. Evaluate choices made by content creators. |
| | | | | |

| | Going Deep |
|---|---|
| | I completed a reflection about a film clip, musical selection, or work of art Using the discussion questions for all media to guide me. |
| | I evaluated the performances of different actors playing the same role. |
| | I created a piece of art in a medium of my choice that represents my feelings About, or an interpretation of Shakespeare's writing. |

The benchmarks for this learning goal were established using the Common Core Standards.

## Assessments

The following prompts increase in complexity and can be used as an assessment tool. Student responses may come in various product forms including a written or spoken response, a student-designed and completed graphic organizer, or a digital presentation using the application of choice.

As you view this scene think about how it is portraying what is in the text. Choose three examples of the media reflecting specific descriptions of the text and explain how the text and media are connected.

As you view this scene, think about how it is adding to the beauty, tone, and meaning of the text. Choose an example of each and explain how the media version contributes to our experience of the text's beauty, tone, and meaning.

After you view this scene, reflect on the experience of viewing the multimedia as compared to simply reading the text. Compare and contrast the two experiences of the text. Give examples as you explain how your experience of the two was similar and different.

As you view this scene, be mindful of different film techniques being used including camera angles, lighting, and music. Compare and contrast the text to the multimedia scene by focusing on the techniques used and how they contribute to your experience of the text and multimedia.

Write a review of a film or cartoon adaptation of the anchor text. Your review should include an analysis of how the film remains true to or departs from the original, and a critique of the techniques used and choices made by the film maker.

## Activities for Exploring Media

Examining interpretations of Shakespeare's texts as presented through the media of art, music, and film provides another avenue for exploring the Bard's work. This chapter features multimedia resources and corresponding discussion questions that work in conjunction with learning goals in other chapters. For instance, watching certain scenes can help clarify comprehension which aligns to the activities in Chapter 2, and multimedia provides a comparison and contrast point to the text which supports the comparing and contrasting work described in Chapter 8. Further, multimedia works can be considered additional texts which can be used to create and support claims made by students as they work with any of the learning goals provided in this resource.

### Discussion Questions for All Media

The following questions address the areas of growth for students when analyzing multimedia. They can be used in conjunction with any of the media resources described below.

### Make Connections

What plot event, or act and scene, is taking place in this clip? What evidence supports your thinking?

How is the clip portraying the setting of the text? What evidence supports your thinking?

### Contribution to Meaning: Tone and Beauty

What do you understand after seeing/hearing this clip that you did not understand as you were reading?

What new understandings did this clip provide?

### Experience

How did this clip/artwork make you feel?

How does this clip differ from what you imagined as you read?

### Techniques

What did you notice about the use of music in this scene?

Why do you think the filmmaker made so many fast edits in this clip?

Why do you think the filmmaker shot this from above/below?

What do you notice about the colors used in this piece of art? Why do you think the artist made those choices with regards to color?

## Evaluate

Compare the actors who performed in each clip. Who do you think did a better job of capturing the character? Why?

Rate how well you think the filmmaker/artist/composer did in capturing the mood of this scene. What led you to that evaluation?

## Versions of *A Midsummer Night's Dream*

There are two film adaptations of *A Midsummer Night's Dream* that I recommend: Max Reinhardt's 1935 film, and Michael Hoffman's 1999 version. The 1935 version is an epic, black and white retelling, while the 1999 version is a visual feast of detail-rich scenes and vibrant color.

### William Shakespeare's *A Midsummer Night's Dream* (1999)

00:00:00–00:12:00 In these opening minutes the setting is established, preparations are being made for the wedding celebration of Hippolyta and Theseus, and we see Egeus, father of Hermia, present his problems to Theseus the Duke. Egeus wants his daughter to marry Demetrius, but Hermia wants to marry Lysander. These opening minutes also introduce the audience to the four main characters: Hermia, Helena, Demetrius, and Lysander. The scene includes enough dialogue from those characters to do an initial compare and contrast.

Has the setting for this version been changed from Shakespeare's original? What clues in the opening make you aware of this?

Why do the flying lights appear at some moments, but not others?

Note Hippolyta's reaction as she leaves the scene. What do you think she might be thinking and what in Theseus's words may have led to that reaction?

What does Lysander mean when he tells Hermia the course of true love never did run smooth?

**00:14:00–00:23:25.** This sequence shows the first meeting of the Mechanicals and helps students understand what the Mechanicals are. The sequence also informs the audience of the setting. Drawing students' attention to the fact that this is set in Italy and Italian cultural elements such as language and opera appear will prepare them to consider staging their performance in a different cultural context as well.

What announcement is hanging in the market square? How are the Mechanicals connected to this announcement?

What details do you notice in this sequence? Why might these details have been included?

Is this version set in an English-speaking country? How do you know? What elements of Italian heritage and culture are present in this scene?

Describe Nick Bottom. What events occur in this clip to support your characterizations?

Notice what the other actors are doing while not speaking. How can you use what you have noticed in the film actor's delivery of lines to improve your own performance?

Why do you suppose this group is called the Mechanicals?

Why did it take Bottom so long to decide to take the part?

What do you notice about the mood of the music as Bottom leaves? Why did the director make this choice?

**00:23:40–00:24:55** In this clip we see a very frustrated Helena trudging through the rain after hearing from Hermia that she and Lysander plan on running away together.

**According to Helena, why is it raining?**

Notice what happens to the music once Helena decides to tell of "fair Hermia's flight." **Why do you think the film maker made that choice?**

Again, the flying lights appear. Why?

As the clip ends, we are led to a new setting. What is the mood of this new setting, and how does the filmmaker use sound to transition the viewer to the new setting's mood?

**00:25:35–00:27:15** In this clip we meet Puck. This scene is a good opportunity to discuss how an actor brings a character to life as we see Stanley Tucci provide Puck with mannerisms and facial expressions that portray his devilish sense of humor.

**Describe Puck. What events occur in this clip to support your characterizations?**

**How does the actor bring Puck's devilish sense of humor to life?**

**00:27:35–00:29:05** Titania and Oberon arrive in the forest to violent thunder and lightning.

**How does the film maker show the anger that exists between Oberon and Titania?**

**00:32:10 – 00:35:00** This clip finds Oberon devising a plan to get revenge against Titania for not relinquishing a child to him. Titania is caring for the child of a friend, and Oberon wants the child to become another servant of his. With Puck's help Oberon plans to put a magic flower juice on Titania's eyes so that she will fall in love with the first thing she sees. Puck's job is to get the flower.

As Oberon reflects on his plan, he sees Helena and Demetrius arguing. Because he is a fairy and loves love, he wants the two to stop quarreling and be in love. This scene is helpful to show because it clarifies these complex plot points.

**How does the actor playing Puck show the audience Puck's sense of humor without speaking?**

**What is Oberon's plan?**

**What are Demetrius and Helena doing in the forest?**

Oberon spends a lot of time observing people and fairies in the forest. Because he is a fairy, we know that he is invisible. However, the actor, not being a magician, cannot become actually invisible. How does the filmmaker solve the problem of making Oberon invisible?

**00:37:05–00:39:30** This clip includes Oberon delivering the lines that begin, "I know a bank where the wild thyme blows…"

and concludes with a sequence that travels through Titania's area of the forest. Oberon delivers directions to Puck regarding the quarrelling couple he saw – Helena and Demetrius. This scene is interesting to watch and analyze because it shows the film maker's interpretation of Oberon's famous words as they are being delivered in the story. An interesting close read involves comparing the text of Oberon's words to how they are depicted in the scene as it leads to a discussion about the film maker's interpretation and artistic choices.

**Evaluate the film maker's interpretation of Oberon's words. Do you think they did a good job capturing Titania's fairy realm? What areas could be improved?**

00:45:00–00:47:15 In this brief scene Puck encounters the bicycle. This is a good scene to show students as it clearly models the fact that film makers are artists who are free to make decisions when interpreting and creating their own version of Shakespeare's story. Since the students are creating their own productions, they too as artists have the same freedom of choice.

**How is Puck faring on his mission to find the couple Oberon instructed him to find?**

**Note Puck's reaction to finding the bicycle. Describe how he responds to seeing the bike. Is this scene in the original play? Why would the film maker include it?**

**How does the actor playing Puck portray Puck's sense of humor in this scene?**

00:50:40–00:58:20 This is the second Mechanicals scene, and it flows in to the scene in which Bottom is turned into a donkey. This scene helps students visualize what happens during this complex plot point, and it provides one answer to how should one stage an invisible fairy, Puck, turning a human into a donkey, Bottom, in the presence of a group of his friends.

**How do the other characters feel about Bottom? How do you know?**

**Think back to the first scene in which we met Bottom. How did you characterize him? Does this scene support that characterization, or provide a new perspective on Bottom?**

**Why do you think Shakespeare decided to turn Bottom into a donkey as opposed to any other animal?**

Note how the film maker uses music in this scene. What purpose does the music serve?

How does the actor portraying Bottom change his performance to support the idea that Bottom has become a donkey?

What do you think of Titania's greeting to Bottom? Is she seeing him clearly? Do people in love see each other clearly?

1:00:50–1:03:35 This scene begins with a tableau of Titania and Bottom in the forest. This is an opportunity to show some of the paintings inspired by *A Midsummer Night's Dream* and to ask students to what degree the film maker may have been inspired by those paintings. Next, Oberon and Puck realize Puck's mistake in placing the love potion on the wrong couple's eyes. This scene is helpful as it helps clarify complex plot points.

1:26:25–01:29:05 This scene takes place right after Hermia, Lysander, Helena and Demetrius are discovered the next morning in the woods by Egeus, Theseus, and Hippolyta. In it, Bottom awakens and reflects on his experience.

How does the setting change in this scene?

What is the significance of the bird's nest and its contents? Why do you think the film maker chose to have Bottom discover those objects?

What does Bottom make of his experience?

1:36:00–02:00:00 In this final scene we see all of the happy couples married on their wedding day. The Mechanicals' play has been chosen by the duke and duchess to be performed.

Summarize the story performed by the Mechanicals. How does this play within a play support the theme of *A Midsummer Night's Dream*?

Why do you think Shakespeare choose Pyramus and Thisbe as the story that the Mechanicals perform?

What do the actors do to make their performance of Pyramus and Thisbe, a very sad story of miscommunication, funny rather than tragic?

Consider how you have characterized Bottom in his previous scenes. Has he changed? Or is there more evidence to support your previous characterization of him? What evidence from the scene supports your thinking?

Who was genuinely the best actor in the Mechanicals? What evidence in the scene supports your thinking?

**01:51:45–02:00:00** This is the final scene in which Puck delivers his final lines and the film maker shows Bottom reflecting once again.

Why did the filmmaker choose to have Puck deliver his last lines from the town and not from the forest?

What do you think Bottom is thinking as he stares out the window?

### *A Midsummer Night's Dream* (1935)

This film is a gorgeous black and white version starring Mickey Rooney and Olivia de Havilland. Scenes can be selected to compare and contrast with the major scenes outlined in the 1999 version. The juxtaposition of the two provides an opportunity to discuss how film making has changed especially with regards to special effects.

## Versions of *Romeo and Juliet*

There are many, many versions of *Romeo and Juliet*. In fact, Wikipedia offers a listing of adaptations that is more than 200 entries long. In my work, I have most frequently shown clips from Baz Luhrmann's 1996 film *Romeo + Juliet*. In addition, the Zeffirelli version of *Romeo and Juliet* from 1968 is another choice from which to add clips to compare to the Luhrmann version. These two films, shown in side by side clips, illustrate for students the range at which Shakespeare can be performed. Zeffirelli gives us the version we expect: ye olde outfits featuring lots of tights worn in a Verona filled with architecture of the Middle Ages, whereas Luhrmann gives us a Verona more like modern Los Angeles featuring Capulets in Hawaiian shirts. Comparing these two visions of the story seems to also give students the freedom to begin imagining Shakespeare as their own. That is imagining a Shakespeare that is speaking to their time and experience.

Aside from the Luhrmann and Zeffirelli films there are several other options for multimedia viewing and corresponding activities. Touchstone Pictures' 2011 film *Gnomeo and Juliet*, the series of animated versions of Shakespeare's tales from the BBC, and several older animations are appropriate to share in their entirety with a class. Lastly, *West Side Story* (either the 2021 version or the 1961), while not necessarily appropriate for all audiences due to violence, can make for excellent compare and contrast discussion – even if specific clips are selected to be shown rather than the whole.

### Baz Luhrmann's *Romeo + Juliet*

This 1996 adaptation of *Romeo and Juliet* is as thrilling as versions of Shakespeare come with colorful scenes and young modern players set to a soundtrack of rock that will resonate with students. Thrilling as it is though, there are some scenes and content which may not be suitable for a school audience due to language, sexuality, or substances. However, I have outlined the scenes below that exclude the most controversial content yet reveal a film maker's perspective on the Romeo and Juliet that students may find illuminating and inspiring to the creation of their own productions.

    00:00:00–00:09:45 During this portion of the film the audience experiences the prologue as if it were a newscast. We meet the Capulets and the Montagues as roving groups of young men looking for trouble in a Verona that resembles present day Los Angeles. The Montagues are dressed in Hawaiian shirts while the Capulets are attired in deep velvets. Their arrivals are marked by different music which increases in intensity as the exchange of insults between the two groups ratchets tensions higher and higher. The chaos and feeling of impending doom are further emphasized by the quick camera cuts that make one feel slightly ill as they watch. The tense exchange grows at a gas station, and ignites a major conflict which forces the prince, in the film the police chief of Verona, to proclaim that further violence will lead to death.

    **Compare and contrast the way the Capulets and Montagues are portrayed in the opening scenes. What similarities and differences do you notice? Why do you think the film maker might have made those choices? What text evidence supports or refutes the choices made?**

**Compare the opening scenes of Luhrmann's** *Romeo + Juliet* **with Zeffirelli's** *Romeo and Juliet.* **What do you notice about the settings, characters, and conflicts in these two styles?**

**What is the mood of this scene? How does the filmmaker use different techniques to affect the mood and tension?**

**How does Luhrmann adapt** *Romeo + Juliet* **for modern times while also honoring Shakespeare's original language?**

This scene is an outstanding example of how film makers have reimagined the staging of *Romeo and Juliet* and how Shakespeare can be adapted for modern times. One example of how Baz Luhrmann connected the Shakespearean text to a modern setting is with guns instead of swords. To keep the connection to the text, however, he included close ups of the guns to show engravings which name the weapons as Shakespeare did. For example, in the original text Lord Montague asks for his longsword, and at this moment in the film the camera flashes to a large gun on a display shelf that is engraved with the name: Longsword. Luhrmann knew swords would be nonsensical in modern Los Angeles, but guns would fit the time more closely. Prince is a police officer. I have found that students are not comfortable making the content their own unless they see proof that it has been done before.

**00:10:25–00:11:20** In this scene we first meet Romeo and understand how Baz Luhrmann will characterize him. As the camera cuts from a far shot to a close up, we see Romeo is smoking. Students often see the smoking as further evidence of his poor decision-making skills.

**Compare how Romeo is characterized when we first meet him to how his cousins are portrayed in the first 10 minutes. What is the same? Different? Consider music, lighting, color, etc. How do these decisions shape how the audience sees Romeo compared to his cousins?**

**00:13:35–00:14:10** In this clip we first see a modernized portrayal of Paris. Luhrmann first shows Paris, here Dave Paris, as the cover face on *Timelet Magazine*'s Bachelor of the Year issue.

**Explain how Baz Luhrmann characterizes and modernizes Paris. Why do you think he made these decisions?**

**00:26:00–00:30:30** This scene is the one in which Romeo and Juliet meet, Juliet meets Paris, and Romeo and Juliet discover they are members of opposing families. Because the sequence is largely dialogue free, and skillfully performed, there are many opportunities for alter ego writing or in role writing as the actor's gestures and facial expression allow for inferences to be made. Notice how the music changes between 32:00 and 33:30.

**The music in this scene changes dramatically. Why? How does the change in music inform the viewer's understanding of the realization just made by Romeo and Juliet?**

**What do you think Paris, Romeo, and Juliet are all thinking throughout this sequence?**

**00:36:00–00:40:25** This is the famous balcony scene. It is worth watching if students are having a hard time visualizing this exchange between Romeo and Juliet.

**00:46:55–00:49:35** Romeo meets with Friar Lawrence to explain his situation with Juliet and to ask if the Friar will marry them.

**Friar Lawrence is contemplating a conflict when we meet him. What is he contemplating? What type of conflict is he experiencing? How is this a conflict?**

**Consider the song choice at 48:45. Explain why this song was chosen. What effect does it have on the mood of the scene? How does it echo the theme of the text?**

**00:53:05–00:57:30** This scene is worth watching because it clarifies some plot points that may be unclear to students. In these minutes we see a conversation between Romeo and the Nurse in which Romeo tells her that he and Juliet will be married by Friar Lawrence in the morning. Next we see a humorous conversation between the Nurse and Juliet in which Juliet begs to hear Romeo's message. Finally we see the wedding.

**00:58:30–1:10:40** This is the murder of Mercutio and Tybalt scene. This scene can also be compared with the same scene in Zeffirelli's version.

**1:12:20–1:15:15** In this scene we see a devastated Romeo seek Friar Lawrence's help after being banished from Verona for the murder of Tybalt.

**What does this scene reveal about Romeo's maturity level?**

**1:22:10–1:26:40** Juliet is told by Lord and Lady Capulet that she will marry Paris on Thursday. This is a great scene to watch prior to debating the question: How much control or decision making power should parents and guardians have over the lives of their children? Further, if viewed in conjunction with Ophelia's scenes in *Hamlet*, opportunities for character to character comparison arise.

**Compare the points of view of the nurse, Lord Capulet, Lady Capulet, and Juliet with regards to Juliet marrying Paris.**

**1:26:40–1:27:50** In this scene, Paris is speaking with Friar Lawrence when Juliet arrives. Juliet is hoping to seek the Friar's support with her husband problem. At this point she is married to Romeo, but has been directed to marry Paris. This provides an opportunity to compare and contrast Juliet and Paris's points of view in the moment. This scene can also be used in conjunction with Rome's visit to the Friar so that Romeo and Juliet's response to adverse circumstances can be compared.

**What are the three perspectives in this scene – said versus unsaid in role writing – what are the characters thinking?**

**Compare Juliet's visit to the Friar with Romeo's visit. What can we learn about the characters from the similarities and differences in their interaction with the Friar in these scenes?**

**1:30:00–1:31:35** In this scene we see Juliet in conflict.

**Evaluate the amount of time Juliet spent making the decision she makes in this scene. Do you agree or disagree with her choice?**

**What type of conflict is Juliet experiencing? What are the opposing arguments on each side?**

**How do music transitions affect how this scene is felt as a viewer versus felt as a reader?**

**1:32:00–1:37:35** In this scene Balthasar leaves the church after drawing incorrect conclusions. Balthasar leaves without all of the information, so that actions are taken without all knowledge. This is an excellent scene to demonstrate the theme of either unintended consequences or the perils of acting without a full understanding. Had Balthasar gathered all of the details prior to taking action, then the miscommunication that led to Romeo and Juliet's deaths might have been avoided.

## Franco Zeffirelli's 1968 *Romeo and Juliet*

I show scenes from Zeffirelli's film so that students have an opportunity to compare and contrast the creative and interpretive choices made by actors and film makers. Having two clips of the same scene as created by two different minds lets students analyze and evaluate artistic choices and evaluate the effectiveness of those choices. A simple way to engage students in such an activity would be to analyze, then compare and contrast the opening of Zeffirelli's *Romeo and Juliet* with the opening of Baz Luhrmann's *Romeo + Juliet*. Other scenes which make excellent resources for analysis and comparison include the scene in which Juliet consults with her nurse after her nurse meets with Romeo, and the wedding scene because they allow students to examine and evaluate the choices made by both the actress and the film makers.

## *West Side Story*

The film *West Side Story*, both the 1954 and the 2021 versions, are based directly on *Romeo and Juliet*. Two members of opposing gangs, the Jets and the Sharks, fall in love. This film provides excellent opportunities for comparing and contrasting, as well as providing an example for how Shakespeare's stories have been reinterpreted over time.

## Additional Versions

- *Gnomeo and Juliet* (2011).
    This animated version featured Romeo and Juliet as garden gnomes. Set in Shakespeare's birthplace of Stratford Upon Avon, the Capulets and Montagues in this version are at war over who are the better gardeners.
- *Shakespearean Spinach* (1940).
    Popeye stars as Romeo and Olive Oyl as Juliet in this seven-minute cartoon short in which Bluto tries to sabotage their love. While there is not a ton of depth to this short, it does provide another example for students to see that their own decisions regarding staging the text are entirely valid.

## Versions of *Hamlet*

Like *Romeo and Juliet*, *Hamlet* has been adapted countless times. Of those adaptations, the versions that I like for students to see sample clips of to compare and support comprehension and analysis are the 1996 Kenneth Branagh version and the 2000 version by Michael Almereyda. The 1996 version is unabridged and set in 19th-century Denmark. By contrast, the 2000 version is set in modern day New York City in which the country of Denmark is replaced by the Denmark Corporation. Finally, Disney's *The Lion King* is an animated retelling of *Hamlet* in which the characters are animals of the African savannah.

### *Hamlet* (1996)

00:00:00–00:04:30 In this scene, Marcellus, Horatio, and Bernardo see the ghost. Horatio was initially skeptical that there even was a ghost to be seen until his friends forced him to stay and see for himself. This scene is important for students to watch because it orients them to the setting and mood, while also orienting them to the central conflict and providing evidence for one side of an essential question central to the plot: Is Hamlet communicating with the ghost of his father? Also, seeing that a ghost will be at the center of classroom debate is engaging for students!

**What mood is the director trying to inspire? What tools does he use to create mood? How effective are those tools?**

**What do you understand about the setting that you did not previously understand having just read the text? Is the film maker updating the text in any way? How do you know?**

00:14:55–00:21:55 In this scene we meet Hamlet for the first time. We see how he interacts with Claudius and Gertrude on their wedding day, and how his demeanor contrasts with the festive mood of the day.

**Compare Hamlet's appearance to the setting in general. Does Hamlet fit in with his surroundings? What makes you draw that conclusion? Why would the film maker make that choice?**

**What do you infer Hamlet is feeling as he listens to Polonius' speech about death? What is he thinking to himself?**

What do you think the people of the court are thinking as they watch Polonius and Gertrude ask Hamlet not to return to school in Wittenburg?

What do you think Hamlet is thinking as the confetti falls?

After he is alone Hamlet gives his first soliloquy. Explain, to the best of your knowledge, what he is thinking.

00:27:45–00:32:35 In this scene we see the conversation between brother and sister, Laertes and Ophelia, and then between father and son, Polonius and Laertes. Advice is given by Laertes to Ophelia and by Polonius to Laertes. This is a helpful scene to watch as seeing and hearing those lengthy speeches delivered can bring additional layers of comprehension. In an analysis of how Ophelia changes over time, this scene can serve as a text as it shows Ophelia with a sense of humor and intact intellect as evidenced by the fact that she recognizes the hypocrisy in Laertes' advice to her.

00:37:00–00:51:00 In this scene Horatio and Marcellus take Hamlet to see the ghost. This is a fun scene to watch with students because it is full of tense arguments and, of course, a ghost. Prior to watching, try having the students write or act out a sketch in which one friend wants to follow a ghost beckoning them into the woods. Write or improvise the scene in which all of the friends respond. After taking a brief or extended time to do this in role imagining, view the scene up until 39:00. Then, you can discuss how their versions of the scene were different or similar. From 39:00–45:45 we see the conversation between the ghost and Hamlet. We see what Hamlet imagines as the ghost speaks. The inclusion of this scene also provides additional text for analyzing Hamlet as it shows him interacting with the ghost alone. Because he is conversing with the ghost alone it begs the question: Is Hamlet imagining the interaction?

What effect do Hamlet's flashbacks have on how he hears the ghost's words?

Who is narrating the flashbacks? How do you know?

Once Marcellus and Horatio find Hamlet, the ghost appears again. What evidence is there in the scene that Horatio and Marcellus see or hear the ghost?

**01:07:50–01:10:40** After discussing Hamlet's behavior with Polonius and discovering that his strange behavior may be the result of Ophelia, Polonius plans to speak with him. In this scene Polonius confronts Hamlet to try and determine what is making him act so strangely. The conversation provides text to explore the question of whether or not Hamlet has lost his mind or if, as Polonius says, "there is method to his madness."

**Describe Hamlet's attitude in this scene. How is he similar or different from how he appeared in the previous scene?**

**Does Hamlet have his wits about him or has he lost his mind? What evidence from the scene supports your thinking?**

**What is Hamlet's opinion of Polonius? What evidence from the text supports your claim?**

**1:12:35–1:19:50** – In this scene we see Hamlet first greet his friends Rosencrantz and Guildenstern with joy. However, joy transitions to doubt and irritation as Hamlet wonders why they have arrived and who sent them. Hamlet's tone changes once again as he works to get the truth out of them. Finally, the tone dramatically changes once more as Hamlet reflects on the nature of man in his "What a piece of work is man" soliloquy. Then the trio discuss the theater group that is coming to visit and Hamlet's tone changes yet again to that of an enthusiastic leader. As the trio enter the palace, they encounter Polonius which leads to another series of tone changes. In the final tone change of the sequence, we see Hamlet return to the enthusiastic leader tone. This scene, in conjunction with the other scenes in which Rosencrantz and Guildenstern appear, is an additional text for exploring the theme of friendship within *Hamlet*. This scene can also work to support a close read of Hamlet's "What a piece of work is man" soliloquy. Finally, it is an excellent text for determining whether or not Hamlet is mad as we get to see his mood change repeatedly throughout the scene.

**Note how Hamlet's mood changes throughout this scene. Describe any changes in tone that you recognize. What do these changes tell you about how Hamlet feels?**

**1:30:40–01:31:50** This scene opens with Rosencrantz and Guildenstern sharing their conversation with Hamlet to Claudius. It is an excellent piece of secondary text to add to the above scene because it provides evidence that the two childhood friends are deceiving Hamlet.

**Are Rosencrantz and Guildenstern good friends to Hamlet? Evaluate the friendship that Rosencrantz and Guildenstern offer Hamlet. Support your claim with evidence from the scene or text.**

Note how the camera moves in this scene. Describe the movement. Why would the film maker choose to shoot this scene this way?

**1:37:50–1:40:50** This scene provides evidence that Hamlet is either going insane or is quite sane. In this scene we see Ophelia return letters that Hamlet wrote her, and which Polonius had found in her room, back to Hamlet. The scene is a study in how an actor can portray a character dealing with a person versus self conflict with facial expressions alone.

Note how this scene was shot. Are there more close shots or long shots? Why would the film maker choose to shoot this scene this way?

How does Hamlet change in this scene? How does the actor playing Hamlet help us notice his change?

**1:49:15–2:04:05** This scene begins with Hamlet asking Horatio for help, and continues into the performance of the play organized by Hamlet. This scene shows the reactions that the characters have to the play, and provides an excellent secondary text to examine the following question: **Polonius earlier said that there was "method to his madness." He was speaking about Hamlet. Consider the original text as well as character reactions in the film. What do you think Polonius meant what he said that there was "method" to Hamlet's "madness"?**

This scene also provides an excellent opportunity to examine Shakespeare's language deeply by attending to the extended recorder metaphor. The metaphor appears in an exchange with Rosencrantz and Guildenstern and demonstrates Shakespeare's ability to use humor and multiple meanings to insult his rivals and make the text crackle. Kids enjoy deciphering what exactly he is saying. From here, a wonderful connection to rap, and specifically Jay-Z, who like Hamlet uses double meanings to slay his rivals, and often quotes *Hamlet* in his lyrics, can be made. Hamlet, in the recorder metaphor, is almost rapping at Rosencrantz and

Guildenstern in the same way that Jay-Z rapped at Nas during their rivalry.

**2:06:25–2:10:35** In this segment, we see Hamlet vow to "speak in daggers to his mother, but use none" and Claudius reflecting on his deeds in a confessional within a chapel. In this scene Hamlet also struggles with whether or not to kill Claudius as he finds him. This scene demonstrates two concepts: Person versus self conflict, and the effect of setting on character as Hamlet ultimately decides that he cannot kill Claudius as he prays.

**What is the setting of this scene? How does the setting affect Hamlet's person versus self conflict?**

**Notice how the camera moves as Polonius reflects. How is it moving? Why did the filmmaker choose to shoot this scene in that way?**

**2:16:15–2:19:20** In this clip we see Gertrude and Hamlet in conflict. Hamlet has just killed Polonius who lays slain wrapped in a curtain on the ground. The ghost of King Hamlet appears to interrupt their fight.

**Does Gertrude see the ghost of King Hamlet? How do you know?**

**2:47:10–2:51:30** In this scene we see Laertes, returned from school, reuniting with his sister Ophelia. Since he last saw her, she has changed quite a bit due to the loss of their father Polonius and the banishment of Hamlet for his murder.

**Evaluate the actress who plays Ophelia. How does she show Ophelia's changed state of mind? To what extent is she successful in showing us how Ophelia has changed?**

**03:44:00–03:48:14** This scene shows the duel between Laertes and Hamlet, as well as the outcome of Claudius' plan which results in the unintended deaths of Gertrude and Laertes.

Shakespeare is vague in his stage directions, so we know the decision to stage the duel throughout the hall, instead of in one specific place, was a choice the film maker made. Why do you think they chose to shoot the duel as they did?

### *Hamlet* (2000)

*Hamlet* (2000) is a more modern retelling of the story. In this version, Denmark is a corporation that Claudius has taken control of after Hamlet's father's death. An interesting discussion regarding film maker's creative choices can start from the following point: This version of *Hamlet* is 112 minutes long; the 1996 version is over 200 minutes – how can that be? Or, compare and contrast how the film makers handled the scene in which Hamlet and Ophelia's conversation is overheard by Polonius and Claudius? Other scenes in this film that support student exploration and analysis of the Bard are outlined below.

**00:00:00–00:07:40** Opening Sequence

**How is this Denmark different from the Denmark portrayed in the text or *Hamlet* (1996)?**

**How is this version modernized? How is the setting established?**

**Why do you think the film maker chose to have Hamlet be a film maker?**

**14:30–19:35** Polonius gives advice to his son Laertes via his famous neither a borrower or lender be speech.

**Compare and contrast the performance of the two actors playing Polonius in the 1996 version and in the 2000 version.**

**40:15–42:40** Hamlet delivers his "To be or not to be" soliloquy.

**Why did the film maker make the choice to have Hamlet deliver his most serious words in a video store?**

**What does it say about the film maker's opinion of Hamlet that he is saying "to be or not to be" in front of Pringles chips in a video store?**

**Compare and contrast the same scene in the 1996 version of *Hamlet* with this version.**

### *The Lion King*

The Disney hit *The Lion King* is also based on *Hamlet* and makes for a lively comparison and contrast. Similarities include a traitorous uncle, ghostly visits, and a struggle for power over Pride Rock. Differences include the fact that Simba's mother, unlike *Hamlet*'s Gertrude, is a good mother, Simba himself is not going insane, and Nala is a strong character with agency, unlike Ophelia who seems to be a victim of her circumstance.

## Additional Versions of *A Midsummer Night's Dream*, *Romeo and Juliet*, and *Hamlet*

### Shakespeare: The Animated Tales

*Shakespeare: The Animated Tales* is a subtitled and abridged retelling of the stories. The subtitles are invaluable because they let students absorb the text through three modalities simultaneously. They are hearing the text while seeing the images and reading the words. This layering of content supports comprehension. These short versions can be watched in their entirety to compare and contrast with a collection of clips from the feature length films.

### BBC's *Shakespeare in Shorts*

Another wonderful resource is provided on the BBC website. *Romeo and Juliet*, *Hamlet*, and *A Midsummer Night's Dream* are retold in three minutes and set to a gentle rap/pop song that retells the story. This length is suitable for all sorts of activities. First, for students struggling with the general plot, this video can work as a tool for clarification. Students might also be asked to evaluate the summary and video after contemplating what makes an excellent adaptation, and creating a quality adaptation rubric together. Lastly, this video might work as a model should you wish students to create a similar summary – perhaps a live action retelling in three minutes, or a retelling using puppets.

### Activity 1: Analyzing Paintings and Music

Analyzing pieces of art or music related to the texts can work well as a warm up activity between close reading sessions. For instance, if on day one Scenes 1 and 2 are read, prior to beginning Scene 2, a quick write based on an audio clip or a study of a painting can refresh student minds and prepare them to continue reading the text with engagement and improved comprehension. These activities can also be done as predictive pre reading work, in which students reflect on what clues the image provides regarding the plot, or incorporated at other intervals.

The following pieces of art and musical compositions can be found by googling the titles:

## Works of Art

### Works of Art Based on *A Midsummer Night's Dream*

*Scene from A Midsummer Night's Dream* – Edwin Landseer
*Midsummer Eve Painting* – Edward Robert Hughes
*Bottom Asleep* – Sir Hubert von Herkomer
*Hermia and Lysander* – John Simmons
*A Midsummer Night's Dream* – Marc Chagall
*Lysander Declaring His Passion to Helena* – Robert Smirke
*Theseus and Hippolyta Find the Lovers* – Francis Wheatley
*Thisbe* – John William Waterhouse

### Works of Art Based on *Romeo and Juliet*

*The Feigned Death of Juliet* – Lord Leighton Frederic
*Romeo and Juliet: The Tomb Scene* – Joseph Wright of Derby
*The Reconciliation of the Montagues and Capulets over the Dead Bodies of Romeo and Juliet* – Lord Leighton Frederic
*Sketch for the Passions: Love* – Richard Dadd
*Juliet (The Blue Necklace)* – John William Waterhouse

### Works of Art Based on *Hamlet*

*Ophelia* – Sir John Everett Millais
*Ophélie au Milieu des Fleurs* – Odilon Redon
*Hamlet and His Mother* – Eugène Delacroix
*Portrait of Hamlet* – William Morris Hunt
*Hamlet and Ophelia* – Dante Gabriel Rossetti
*The Play Scene in Hamlet* – Daniel Maclise

## Musical Compositions

### Classical Musical Compositions Based on *A Midsummer Night's Dream*

*A Midsummer Night's Dream* – Felix Mendelssohn (1826)
*The Fairy Queen* – Henry Purcell (1692)
*A Midsummer Night's Dream* – Benjamin Britten (1960)
*The Midsummer Marriage* – Michael Tippett (1955)

Classical Musical Compositions Based on *Romeo and Juliet*

*Romeo and Juliet* – Sergei Prokofiev (1935)
*Romeo and Juliet* – Pyotr Ilyich Tchaikovsky (1880)
*Roméo et Juliette* – Hector Berlioz (1839)

Pop Songs with References to *Romeo and Juliet*

*Romeo and Juliet* – Dire Straits
*Love Story* – Taylor Swift

Classical Musical Compositions Based on *Hamlet*

*Hamlet Overture* – Niels Wilhelm Gade (1861)
*Hamlet Overture* – Pyotr Ilyich Tchaikovsky (1888)
*Hamlet Overture* – Franz Liszt (1858)

Pop Songs with References to *Hamlet*

*Ophelia* – The Band
*Hey There Ophelia* – MC Lars
*Marcy Me* – Jay-Z

## Considerations

An aspect of this book that has troubled me is the issue of representation in the various media resources provided in this chapter. The creators of the films, nearly all composers and artists are white and male. One way this might be addressed is inspired by Shonda Rhimes' Netflix series *Bridgerton* and its spin-off *Queen Charlotte*. Among many other projects, Shonda Rhimes has tapped into our cultural love of stories inspired by European monarchies with these two storylines – despise the mass exclusion such stories have historically entailed, and the effects of colonialism that such stories have celebrated. It is problematic if we allow ourselves to be caught up in the swell of costume, architectural glory and gossiping, and scheming and romance at the expense of reality – namely, loving costume without acknowledging that such refined lives were the result of colonialism's violence and theft. Not to mention that no people of color are represented in such stories. Until Shonda. Shonda Rhimes adapted her works of historical fiction, which allow us to feast on all of the beauty of a setting that has been modernized in terms of racial representation and language. Why can't we point this representational imbalance out to our students and give them the power to create and compose as well? This could be an excellent addition to the students' Shakespeare Festival. Here is language you might consider using to explain a creative project.

Although more modern interpretations and references to Shakespeare are made by artists like Jay-Z and Taylor Swift, the majority of these pieces, artwork, films, and musical compositions are all interpretations of Shakespeare through the eyes of mostly white men. While the lens of white men is one important perspective, there is a vast number of other important perspectives to be considered. What might women, people of other cultures, the youth of another time, you and your peers, those who speak English as a second or third or 19th language have to add to the robust body of creation inspired by Shakespeare? What might creators with different perspectives have to say about Shakespeare's work? How might they interpret it within another media? Aside from painting and classical music, what other media might serve a reinterpretation well? These questions can help students begin to conceive a creative endeavor of their own to add to their Shakespeare Festival.

> What might women, people of other cultures, the youth of another time, you and your peers, those who speak English as a second or third or 19th language have to add to the robust body of creation inspired by Shakespeare?

## Revisiting Essential Unit Question

### What Is the Power of Language?

During this exploration of the essential question, ask students to consider how music and art are like languages. How has the power of the language of art or music been evidenced? Insights will be found in discussions that investigate how the multimedia version contributes to the beauty and meaning of a text. For instance, Purcell's *Fairy Queen* inspires a feeling of regal magic that signals with intensity just how majestic Titania is. The music gives the reader an impression of her that may not be conveyed by the text alone. From such a conversation students begin to conclude that the arts are a powerful language which can express emotion in a way that words alone cannot.

## Film Resources

Allers, R. (Director), & Minkoff, R. (Director). (1994). *The Lion King*. Buena Vista Pictures.

Almereyda, M. (Director). (2000). *Hamlet 2000*. Miramax.

Asbury, K. (Director). (2001). *Gnomeo and Juliet*. Touchstone Pictures.

BBC. (2023, May 24). *Shakespeare in shorts*. https://www.bbc.co.uk/programmes/articles/4w5xvV324jx463XyCyctnBs/shakespeare-in-shorts

Branagh, K. (Director). (1996). *Hamlet*. Columbia Pictures.

Garfield, L. (Director). (1992). *Shakespeare: The animated tales*. Dave Edwards Studio.

Hoffman, M. (Director). (1999). *A midsummer night's dream*. Fox Searchlight Pictures.

Luhrmann, B. (Director). (1996). *Romeo + Juliet*. Twentieth Century Fox.

Manuell, G. (Director). (1940). *Shakespearean spinach*. Paramount Pictures.

Reinhardt, M. (Director), & Dieterle, W. (Director). (1935). *A midsummer night's dream*. Warner Brothers.

Spielberg, S. (Director). (2021). *West side story*. Amblin Entertainment.

Wise, R. (Director), & Robbins, J. (Director). (1961). *West side story*. United Artists.

Zeffirelli, F. (Director). (1968). *Romeo and Juliet*. Paramount Pictures.

## References

AACAP. (n.d.). *Screen time and kids*. https://www.aacap.org/AACAP/Families_and_Youth/Facts_for_Families/FFF-Guide/Children-And-Watching-TV-054.aspx

*Generation M2: Media in the lives of 8- to 18-year-olds*. (2010, January 1). https://www.kff.org/other/poll-finding/report-generation-m2-media-in-the-lives/

Lamb, C., & Lamb, M. (1807). *Tales from Shakespeare*. Juvenile Library of William Godwin.

National Governors Association Center for Best Practices & Council of Chief State School Officers. (2010). *Common core state standards for English language arts and literacy in history/social studies, science, and technical subjects*. Authors.

Rhimes, S. (Executive Producer). (2020). *Bridgerton*. Netflix.

Rhimes, S. (Executive Producer). (2023). *Queen Charlotte*. Netflix.

Shakespeare, W. (1596). *A midsummer night's dream*.

Shakespeare, W. (1597). *Romeo and Juliet*.

Shakespeare, W. (1601). *Hamlet*.

# 8
# Comparing and Contrasting

Early in my teaching career, compare and contrast was the learning activity I used on Mondays after a long weekend of too much fun and not enough planning on my end. The reason was because of the low amount of preparation required. All too often when assigning a compare and contrast activity, I would simply pull out a Venn diagram and send the kids off and running to list the things that were the same or different between a story we'd read and an accompanying film. Student work was full of less than fascinating similarities and differences they'd found, such as characters being addressed by nicknames or not looking the way they expected. Plot differences were summarized by one brief comment explaining how a scene had been omitted in the film. To say the least, the thinking the students were doing on these occasions was a not breaking any brain sweat. They were not my most proud days.

So, instead of feeling cruddy about the work I was doing, I reflected on better ways to do it. In reviewing student writing, I recognized a problem related to parity. Students were not comparing the same types of things across texts. I needed to show them how to think in terms of categories of comparison. Otherwise the deepest depth of their thinking would be to say, Text A had this while Text B did not. Followed by Text B had this while Text A did not. I do not mean to say that this type of comparing

> Thinking in terms of categories allows students to process the texts deeply and demonstrate their comprehension more completely.

and contrasting is not valid – it is entirely, however I think it should come in addition to thinking in terms of categories as well. Thinking in terms of categories allows students to process the texts deeply and demonstrate their comprehension more completely.

## Learning Goals

When working with the skill of comparing and contrasting across the continuum, students are working to compare and contrast treatment of themes within texts. As students work across the continuum the definition of text becomes progressively more expansive definition of text. Initially, students work to compare and contrast within texts from the same genre before moving on to compare texts in different genres. Finally, students look to see how different texts fictionalize history, and how texts draw on mythology to inspire themes, characters, and events. Stating learning goals directly will help students identify the purpose of instruction and thus be more likely to achieve it. Specifically, students will be able to compare and contrast to determine how themes, topics, and patterns are handled by different texts.

### Module Learning Goals

| | Going Far | | | | |
|---|---|---|---|---|---|
| | 4 | 5 | 6 | 7 | 8 |
| | Compare and contrast the treatment of similar themes, topics, and patterns of events in stories, myths, and traditional literature from different cultures. | Compare and contrast stories in the same genre on their approaches to similar themes and topics. | Compare and contrast texts in different forms or genres in terms of their approaches to similar themes and topics. | Compare and contrast a fictional portrayal of a time, place, or character and a historical account of the same period as a means of understanding how authors of fiction use or alter history. | Analyze how a modern work of fiction draws on themes, patterns of events, or character types from myths, traditional stories, or religious works such as the Bible, including describing how the material is rendered new. |
| | | | | | |

|  | Going Deep |
| --- | --- |
|  | I found comparisons and contrasts in two different actors' performances of the same character, different directors' creation of the same scene, or similar. |
|  | I found comparisons and contrasts between different versions of the same story. |
|  | I found comparisons and contrasts in the structure of different lines spoken by the same character. |
|  | I rewrote a scene in a comedy as a tragedy, or in a tragedy as a comedy. |

The benchmarks for this learning goal were established using the Common Core Standards.

## Instruction: Assessments

The following prompts increase in complexity and can be used as an assessment tool. Student responses may come in various product forms including a written or spoken response, a student designed and completed graphic organizer, or a digital presentation using the application of choice.

Choose two texts to compare. Text one must be the anchor text. Text two may be:

- A multimedia adaptation or interpretation of Shakespeare's work.
- Another of Shakespeare's stories
- A related story such as a myth or traditional tale like Pyramus and Thisbe.

Then, compare and contrast the two texts to explain:

- Similarities in theme topic, and patterns.
- Differences in theme topic and patterns.
- How authors of fiction use or alter history.
- How the material is adapted into something new.

## Activities

The following activities provide ideas for how and what students might compare and contrast. Products for such investigations can always be writing based; however, consider asking the students to design the products themselves. One suggestion for going about this would be to share the assessment prompt and explain to students that as long as they show evidence of finding text backed examples of similarities and differences, the manner in which they do so is up to them. Examples might be a video based answer, an animation, a speech, an audio recording of their analysis, or even a performance or piece of artwork with oral explanation.

## Activity 1: Text to Text Comparing and Contrasting

When comparing and contrasting texts the definition of text needs to be first established. Text in this sense refers to the traditional definition which includes anything that is written as well as anything that offers an interpretation of Shakespeare's works such as a song or film where the words may not be explicitly written out, but rather spoken for the viewer. With this expanded definition of text, students have a plethora of options to compare and contrast in this resource alone. Students might compare the Mary and Charles Lamb adaptations to the edited versions of *Hamlet, Romeo and Juliet,* or *A Midsummer Night's Dream*. Especially tenacious students might be interested in comparing a scene from the edited versions of the original text to the entirety of the same scene in the original text. The BBC cartoon versions might be compared to the live action films; live action film scenes might be compared to original texts, etc. Students have the ability to choose texts to compare and contrast based on their own interests. There are numerous possibilities which is wonderful considering the importance of agency and choice in our classrooms.

**Time:** Two to four class periods
**Materials:**

- Two source texts
- Chart paper

**Steps:**

1. For the purposes of this lesson it is not imperative that students have a spectacular reason for comparing and contrasting because the purpose is to practice ensuring parity in comparison. That is to say that if a student is comparing *A*

*Midsummer Night's Dream* and *Romeo and Juliet*, elements of magic may not be a good category of comparison because there is nothing to compare in Romeo and Juliet as there are no magical elements in the story, thus there is nothing to compare and no deeper contrast to make aside from saying one story features magical elements while the other does not. If, however, we modify the category of comparison to ways characters solved problems instead of magical elements then we definitely have commensurate information: Both stories use plants to solve problems. The category of solving problems could be thought of prior to second readings and viewings, or the information identified – in this case a medicine created by Friar Lawrence from the plants in his garden and a magical flower gathered by Puck – could be united by a post reading sort of identified similarities and differences.

2. Determine how students will establish categories of comparison. The categorization issue can be addressed in one of two ways. The first way requires categories of comparison to be established ahead of reading. The second way requires identified similarities and differences to be categorized after they are gathered.

3. Students engage with the texts through a second reading or viewing in which they seek out information. An effective way to organize this work to maximize motivation and learning is to establish several categories of comparison with students so that students have the experience of seeking evidence to compare using a specific category, but to also allow students to find general areas of compare and contrast to be sorted and categorized after the reading so that they have experience in that methodology as well.

4. Understanding that they are looking for comparisons and contrasts relating to the established categories as well as their own discoveries, send students to annotate the text. Students may complete this reading and annotating in partnerships or independently.

5. Teams should form and gather based on who was searching for information in the same category. First, teams should articulate the evidence that they found into at least one statement

of comparison and or contrast. Then students can move on to determine categories of comparison for other noted similarities and differences. Once the categories and evidence are organized, the information should be noted on the graphic organizer.
6. Teams can then present their findings. As teams share information can be written on a large class sized graphic organizer to consolidate the findings.
7. A follow up lesson might include information about transition words used in compare and contrast pieces. Finally, students can use the class graphic organizer as the basis for a written response to a compare and contrast question.

## Activity 2: Comparing Structures

According to the science of reading research, studying and understanding structure is an avenue to improved comprehension. Within the structure of Shakespeare's works exist a range of comparisons that can be made. First, the simple structural elements of prose, and drama can be identified through direct instruction. Second, characters within *Hamlet*, *Romeo and Juliet*, and *A Midsummer Night's Dream* speak in different structures which can be a basis of comparison. For instance, some lines are delivered in iambic pentameter, while others are delivered in a simple sing song rhyme. Investigating those style choices can yield rich insights about the characters. We know for instance that when Hamlet's lines are structured based on rhyme and short sing song length, as they are when he is speaking with Polonius, then he is usually mocking the person to whom he is speaking. However, his serious soliloquies are speeches in iambic pentameter in which he contends with questions of morality. Why would Shakespeare structure those two instances of a character speaking so differently? Second the structure of genre might be applied as a point of comparison. *A Midsummer Night's Dream* is a comedy and *Romeo and Juliet* and *Hamlet* are tragedies. It is interesting to see how the different genres of the three plays handle similar themes. Lastly, since there are different structures applied in film than in the writing of a drama or prose, so comparing the film to drama or prose or live action theater is a third strand of comparison that can be made.

## Comparing the Structure of Drama Versus Story

Dramas and stories written in prose have different structures entirely. Students may benefit from a direct instruction lesson in which they identify those differences, or a group activity in which they examine two artifacts, one drama and one story, and notice and name differences before gathering as a class to formalize their learning via a list or other graphic organizer.

## Comparing the Structures of Comedy Versus Tragedy

Comedies and tragedies have different elements that makes them what they are. In general, comedies are lighthearted and have a happy ending in which conflicts are resolved. They contain larger than life characters in absurd situations with plenty of puns, wit, and sarcasm to make the audience laugh. In comedies characters, who are highly relatable, often get what they deserve. This is perfectly illustrated by *A Midsummer Night's Dream*'s Mechanicals. The Mechanicals desperately want to be appreciated as actors, and since they are a lovable and hardworking troop they get what they deserve in the end. They get the esteem of performing in front of the duke and duchess. Bottom, who is the most arrogant of the Mechanicals, speaks over the leader, and insists that only he could be the best at each part, is a bit of an ass, so he literally gets what he deserves when Puck turns him into a donkey! The audience is left feeling happy that true love won and rude behavior was chastised. Dramas, on the other hand, set out to evoke pity and fear on the part of the audience in response to character's struggle and suffering. Tragedies are led by heroes who are worthy of admiration and are for the most part good, but whose downfall is the result of their own choices. Romeo and Juliet, as well as Hamlet, are essentially good people. Romeo and Juliet are champions of true love, while Hamlet could be characterized as a loyal son. However, Hamlet's obsession with revenge, and Romeo and Juliet's jumping to conclusions and failure to think things through, eventually lead to their demise. Readers or theater goers experience pain and sadness at the waste of their lost lives.

After distinguishing the differences and identifying text evidence that confirms the traits exist within the work, students may be ready to show their learning in a creative way – especially after direct instruction. In this case, students might wish to rewrite *Romeo and Juliet* or *Hamlet* as a comedy, and *A Midsummer Night's Dream* as a tragedy. Final products may take the form of simple written stories, written dramas, short films, animations, comic book drawings or other student designed projects.

## *Comparing the Structure of Characters' Lines*

Throughout the texts, students might notice that the cadence of the lines is different from scene to scene or actor to actor. For instance, in *Hamlet*, Polonius is long winded whereas Claudius is more to the point. In *A Midsummer Night's Dream*, Bottom and Puck speak in singsong rhyme, whereas Oberon and Titania speak in long flowing passages. Two of Shakespeare's most famous lines – "To be, or not to be; that is the question" from *Hamlet*, and "But soft! What light through yonder window breaks?" from *Romeo and Juliet* – are both written using the structure of iambic pentameter, but a closer examination reveals that there is a slight difference in the structure. The lines in *Romeo and Juliet* follow the traditional definition of iambic pentameter: Five sets of two syllables, one soft, the next firm. This makes sense as the structure follows the function of what Romeo is saying. In confessing his love we can imagine that his heart is beating in completed sets of iambs – like a heartbeat. *Ta TUM, ta TUM, ta TUM, ta TUM, ta TUM*. As Romeo confesses his feelings we are with him in his feelings because he is speaking in a heartbeat pattern. In *Hamlet*, however, the idea that iambic pentameter represents the heart takes a different turn. In his famous line "To be, or not to be; that is the question," Hamlet contemplates the worth of being alive and finds it lacking. He is contemplating whether it is worthwhile to carry on with the struggle of being alive. The structure of his words reflects his feelings. In this famous opening line we get five sets of iambs as expected, but in the second half ("that is the question") there is an extra syllable: the line therefore has eleven syllables and not ten. *Ta TUM, ta TUM, ta TUM, ta TUM, ta* TUM, *ta*... In this line it is as if the heartbeat has stopped. Once again through structure, Shakespeare is putting us into the experience of the characters. The following lesson outlines how the above information might be experienced by students in class and is based on a lesson that I had originally viewed in video form on the Folger Shakespeare website over a decade ago. That lesson was modeled for high school students, while this is adapted for a younger audience.

**Time:** One class session, plus additional time if including a writing component.

**Materials:**

- Iambic pentameter card set.

**FIGURE 8.1** Students represent the soft and strong sound pairs of 5 iambs.

Note: In this chapter, an engraving of Shakespeare's face by Charles Droeshout (1623) has been used to protect children's identities in photographs.

**Steps:**

1. Establish the reason for comparing and contrasting, as well as the categories of comparison. In this activity the use of

a structure called iambic pentameter will be compared and contrasted to determine how and why Shakespeare would apply such rules to his writing.
2. If possible gather two student volunteers. One volunteer should hold the "ta" poster, and the other the "TUM" poster. Instruct students to read their cards one right after the other. The "ta" student should read their poster gently and softly, while the "TUM" poster-holder should read their card with a strong and louder voice. As students to repeat their reading of their cards several times. Ask the class what this sounds like, but do not reveal the answer by confirming any guesses at this point to allow the anticipation to build.
3. Inform students that the "ta" and "TUM" together are considered an iamb. An iamb is a set of syllables, one soft and one strong. Ask them to apply root knowledge to predict what pentameter means. Some students will make the connection that pent means five and meter has something to do with measuring which will lead some to understand that iambic pentameter is a set of five pairs of soft and strong syllables. At this point ask for eight more volunteers and organize them in a row with their "ta" and "TUM" posters facing the class. Point out that the five sets of iambs represent a line of iambic pentameter. Have the volunteers read their cards in succession several times. Once they read it smoothly, ask the class again what the line of iambic pentameter sounds like. Again, do not reveal the answer. My go to response for maintaining suspense regardless of what the students say at this point is, "Interesting idea! I wonder why Shakespeare would want his work to sound that way."
4. Next, suggest that the class look at some actual lines instead of nonsense sounds. At this point, ask for 10 new volunteers and distribute the posters that have the But soft lines separated into hard and soft syllables. For example, the first two students representing the first iamb will hold the cards "But" and "SOFT" respectively. The second two will hold "what" and "LIGHT" and so on. Each pair will actually have two sets of iambs to read so that two lines can be examined together. Ideally, 20 volunteers is the best, but 10 works if each pair

goals twice. This will result in the following two lines to be read as indicated:

*But SOFT – what LIGHT – through YON – der WIN – dow BREAKS?*
   *It IS – the EAST – and JU – liet IS – the SUN!*

5. As the students read the line in the soft and strong exaggerated rhythm ask the class to simply listen and consider why Shakespeare would have structured Romeo's lines in such a way. Such a conversation might go something like this:

*Teacher:* Do you hear anything familiar yet? Listen to the sounds of our classmates delivering Romeo's line.
*Student:* It sounds like an instrument!
*Teacher:* Interesting idea! I wonder what instrument and why Shakespeare would want Romeo to speak like that. Of course we are exaggerating in this lesson to help us identify the pattern. Let's think. What is going on with Romeo in this scene and what might he be feeling?
*Student:* He liiiiikes Juliet. He kissed her and he thinks she's prettier than Rosaline.
*Student 2:* And when we talk about our most intense feelings – like love – we get nervous.
*Teacher:* Ahhhh ha! Okay, so let's think about that! What happens in our bodies when we are nervous?
*Student:* Our heart beats fast and hard!!! It's like we can hear it!
*Teacher:* YES! So again, why would Shakespeare have Romeo speak in the form of a heartbeat?

At this point, a free for all of energized shouts takes over our formerly composed discussion. Students are just so excited to realize and be able to articulate that Shakespeare has Romeo speak in a heartbeat pattern because he wants the reader to feel like Romeo in that moment. After, the class considers a set of lines written in iambic pentameter from *Hamlet*. The lines from *Hamlet* provide a perfect contrast and allow students to examine why the same structure was applied slightly differently.

6. To explore contrasting lines of iambic pentameter written for Hamlet, gather new volunteers, or in a smaller group keep the ones you have. Distribute the posters that have the line To be or not to be that is the question printed on them in iambs. The first student pair, representing the first iamb "To BE," followed by the second pair holding "or" and "NOT" etc. until the fifth pair holds the cards reading "the" and QUES. At this point I like to make a big deal out of having one poster left. The "tion" poster that completes the word question does not have a student or another syllable of the line to make it a complete iamb. The conversation used to make sense of this extra syllable might go as follows:

*Teacher:* Oh dear. We have an orphan. A left over syllable. Let's see what this will sound like, and as we do, please think of the discussion we had about Romeo that helped us decipher the deeper meaning and purpose in the structure of his line.
   (*The student volunteers read through the line several times while the class simply listens.*)
*Teacher:* Can anyone tell me what Hamlet is talking about in the line: To be or not to be that is the question?
*Student:* Well, he's got a question. I know that.
*Teacher:* Absolutely. Good point. He is asking a question. A question about what?
*Student:* Being.
*Teacher:* Okay. What does THAT mean?
*Student:* What does it mean to just be?
*Teacher:* Yes, I guess that is what I am asking. What does it mean to just, be?
*Student:* To breathe. To go through life.
*Student 2:* Or a day.
*Teacher:* Okay, so with this information, can we better develop Hamlet's question? What is he asking?
*Student:* Is it worth it to go through life?

> *(The teacher asks if students agree or disagree, to gather other perspectives so that the class can reach consensus over the meaning of Hamlet's question.)*

*Teacher:* Okay, so we all somewhat agree that Hamlet is asking about whether life is worth it. Now let's think on Shakespeare who is writing this character contemplating life. Why would he start the lines in iambic pentameter and then just change it up all of the sudden?

*Student:* Because Hamlet isn't sure…

*Teacher:* Interesting thought! That is something to explore in our discussion. Before we explore that idea, I'd like us to revisit what we learned from our Romeo conversation. What did we discover the iambic pentameter sounded like?

> *(This is a great opportunity to have the whole class repeat the "ta TUM" pattern. Half the class can be "ta" and the other half "TUM.")*

*Student:* The heartbeat.

*Teacher:* YES! What happens to the heartbeat in this instance?

*Student:* It gets stopped.

*Student 2:* Right in the middle.

*Student 3:* The beat does not complete!

*Teacher:* I see that too! So what? Why do that?

*Student:* Because it's like death!

*Teacher:* Interesting! Why bother reminding anyone about death here?

*Student:* Because that's what Hamlet is talking about!!!

*Student 2:* Shakespeare connected his words to the heart again. Just like Romeo's heart would be beating fast in a love situation, so the words were in a pattern of a heart beating, but now Shakespeare is talking about death, so the heartbeat of the words stop and get interrupted.

*Teacher:* Just like death interrupts life.

*Student:* Mind. Blown.

7. At this point, work with students to synthesize their understanding by asking questions: Why did Shakespeare use iambic pentameter in Romeo's line? Why did he use iambic pentameter in Hamlet's line? What effect does

iambic pentameter have on the reader in each case? How does Shakespeare's use of iambic pentameter in each case differ?
8. Students may conclude this lesson with a 3-2-1 assessment that requires them to list three differences in the use of iambic pentameter in each case, two lines of Shakespeare's iambic pentameter, and one line of their own iambic pentameter.

## Activity 3: Comparing Story Elements

In considering the story elements of character, point of view, setting, conflict, and resolution a number of comparisons can be made between stories. This does not mean that students must study two or more works in their entirety and in depth to be able to make such comparisons. Rather students might compare the anchor text, that is the core work being studied in depth whether it is *Hamlet*, *Romeo and Juliet*, or *A Midsummer Night's Dream*, to one of the remaining stories not being comprehensively studied. This might be done through several paths depending on the time available, as well as student skill level. One option is to have students compare the anchor work with a scene from one of the other dramas, or with film clips related to the specific element being compared and contrasted. Students might also read the Mary and Charles Lamb version of the story in conjunction with scenes from the original text and or corresponding film clips to compare to the anchor text. For particularly high achieving students, reading the entire resources on the story to be compared to the anchor text is another option. Lastly, students needing further challenge may refer to the unedited original text to obtain further evidence not presented in the resources available with this book.

### *Character Versus Character*

*Hamlet*, *Romeo and Juliet*, and *A Midsummer Night's Dream* each have characters who I imagine would have tremendously interesting conversations if we could get them in a room together. It is this scenario that I share with students when asking them to compare and contrast characters. Imagine the characters in a room sharing a Coke and chatting. What would their reaction to each other be? Would they be comfortable or uncomfortable with each other and why? Are they more alike in personality or more different? Comparing Romeo and Hamlet or comparing Ophelia, Juliet, and Hermia or Helena gives students a lot of content with which to work. Other interesting character comparisons include examining the parents in each of the works to see which are the best or worst.

## Point of View

Point of view can be another line of comparison and contrast for students to explore, either as a component of comparing character, or as a separate line of comparison altogether. Looking back at work done in exploring point of view can yield the evidence necessary to jump right to comparing without having to seek out evidence. Students might consider what they discovered in their point of view work, and use that as the basis for comparing viewpoints. Or, conversely, if a student or the class wants to compare a character's point of view in a manner that has yet to be explored, the tools available in the point of view chapter might be used to organize thinking and gather evidence ahead of making comparisons and contrasts.

Media is also an excellent resource for texts needed to make comparisons and contrasts that are compelling to students. There are films that address the perspective of both Ophelia and Rosaline which might be viewed and compared to the points of view of other characters. To further stretch student thinking, the students might then include their own perspective as a reader/viewer of the situation. For example, a student comparing and contrasting Romeo, Juliet, and Rosaline's points of view might consider the following categories of comparison: Love, going to the Capulets' ball, Romeo and Juliet's marriage. To gather evidence for Rosaline's perspective they might consult the film *Rosaline* (2022) in addition to the texts studied in class. The question they might be working to resolve is this: How do Romeo, Juliet and Rosaline's perspectives on the Capulets' ball, Romeo and Juliet getting married, and love in general compare and contrast? An additional level of difficulty would ask students to include their own perspectives in the comparing and contrasting.

## Conflict and Resolution

Since the themes in each of the anchor stories are similar in that they connect to the greater ideas about friendship, parenting, and problem solving within communities, their conflicts and resolutions are related as well, which opens another compelling avenue of comparison to students. Students can ask, how do the conflicts differ in each of the stories and how were the conflicts resolved? Also, what impact did the resolution have on the characters? For instance, each story is about betrayals within friendship, and within each story is at least one person versus person conflict that exists due to a betrayal within a friendship. Hamlet's relationship with Rosencrantz and Guildenstern is in conflict because the two work to betray Hamlet to his mother and uncle. Hamlet is also in conflict with Ophelia due to a betrayal. In comparison, Hermia and Helena of *A Midsummer Night's Dream* feel betrayed in love by one another. And, if one were to ask Mercutio about his feelings on friendship and betrayal, he might say that he felt betrayed by Romeo's inability to stand up for himself, or at least arrive on time, since he wound up dead at Tybalt's hand after stepping forward to defend Romeo in his absence. Each of these conflicts is similar in that they include a betrayal, but how are those betrayals different? How were they handled by both friends, and how successfully were they resolved? We're the outcomes successful for all involved?

## Settings

In comparing settings students might find it interesting to refer to research they may have done in conjunction with a project outlined in Chapter 3: Story Elements. The project asked students to research the actual places that Shakespeare's settings are inspired by: Verona, Italy; Denmark; or Athens, Greece. In order to explore how a fictional portrayal of a time and place compares to a historical account of the same period, students can compare the details of setting as discovered through their research to how Shakespeare recreated them in his stories. For example, in *A Midsummer Night's Dream* Egeus, Hermia's father, and Theseus, the Duke of Athens, have the power to put Hermia to death for her disobedience regarding who she will marry. Either she does what she is told, or she is executed! This is the circumstance of the setting Hermia lives within. In comparison, students might wonder about the role of girls in Verona or Denmark. During the time of the plays did girls in those locations have more or less power than girls in Athens? Is this just a situation that Shakespeare imagined for Hermia or is it actually similar to how life was in Athens for young women during that time? Students might also consider King Hamlet. Denmark and Elsinore Castle are real places; was King Hamlet an actual king?

Another avenue for comparing settings is to examine how various film versions of Shakespeare's texts develop setting, and compare them to settings in the original text, or to each other. For instance, the opening scenes of Baz Luhrmann's *Romeo + Juliet*, set in a cartoonish modern day Los Angeles, are very different from the beginning of Zeffirelli's *Romeo and Juliet*, which is more traditional. Likewise the opening of the 1997 *A Midsummer Night's Dream* and the 2017 *A Midsummer Night's Dream* can be compared and contrasted with the original text or on their own.

## *Theme*

Comparing and contrasting theme requires students to examine how the same theme is addressed by different texts. *A Midsummer Night's Dream, Romeo and Juliet,* and *Hamlet* each deal with similar themes revolving around the topics of love, friendship, and parenting, so there the opportunities to compare and contrast are plentiful. Students seeking to compare themes might analyze what each text is saying about the topic, how the topic affects the characters involved, and what lesson is learned by the characters.

A student seeking to compare how the topic of love is handled thematically between *A Midsummer Night's Dream* and *Romeo and Juliet* might begin by asking what each of the texts is saying about love. It could be concluded by a student that *A Midsummer Night's Dream* is saying that adults cannot stand in the way of true love, while *Romeo and Juliet* is saying that love makes young people distracted and irresponsible. Such a student may further develop their comparison of the theme of love by asking how the characters were affected by the theme. In *Romeo and Juliet*, the main characters died as a result of their beliefs about love, while in *A Midsummer Night's Dream* the characters had to make choices that defied their family's wishes, but with a bit of magic on the side of the young lovers, ultimately the adults failed at getting the children to do what they wanted. Therefore Shakespeare is telling us something about the power of love in *A Midsummer Night's Dream*, but he is warning us of the fact that love can distract us from common sense as well. Finally, in the same comparison, students can also compare the lessons learned by the character as a result of the theme being what it is. In *Romeo and Juliet*, the Montagues and Capulets learned that their feud was an irresponsible reaction to their beliefs about love, and in that way they are similar to their children. In *A Midsummer Night's Dream*, Egeus and the Duke learn that love is more powerful than their commands. Because all three stories share common themes, such an analysis can be done between any two of the stories across the topics of love, friendship, parenting, and solving problems.

## *Considerations*

Consider carefully when working with gifted students the fact of asynchronous development which tells us that areas of the brain do not develop at the same time. This is why we see students in gifted classes who melt down in a puddle of self-defeat when faced with a minor error they made in a math equation but can also write eloquently on the self-selected journal topic "Why We Do Not Want to Be Infinite" in second grade. For this student, asynchronous development was demonstrated in more advanced language development and in emotional skills that need more time to grow.

For others, like Avery, a former student, complex ideas may exist in the brain before expressive language catches up. This leaves such students in a frustrating place of having a beautiful idea in their mind that they do not yet have the skill to share with others through written language.

In assessing students, I had tended to lean heavily on expecting students to express themselves in writing, and I still do because I think writing is an extremely valuable muscle of the intellect that does not get developed without intention. However, Avery taught me that writing is not the best way for some students – especially those who are neurodivergent – to express their level of understanding especially when we get into the complexities and nuance of comparing and contrasting. Please consider allowing students to express their learning in ways that address the standards, but perhaps not in the way you may have imagined. The moment that Avery shifted my paradigm occurred when he was demonstrating his ability to compare and contrast. We were in math class at the time. And he was blurting out an emotional contrast between characters that he had just now discovered a way to explain. Earlier that day, in reading class, we had been working on comparisons and contrasts, but he could not articulate what was in his head, and it had led to him producing nothing but false starts in 45 minutes. In math class we were looking at graphs. The graphing example I gave sparked something in his mind and he immediately asked to come to the board where he graphed two different character's emotional reactions to their conflict over time, and then proceeded to explain how the graphs were similar and different. He pointed to instances where the graph rose and could explain the plot event that caused the change in the character's emotional state. He had given a detailed comparison and contrast which went beyond grade level expectations, and he had also given his colleagues another reason why studying graphs was a worthwhile endeavor. My point in sharing this story is this: Also consider allowing students to express their learning in ways *they* find effective. Sure, sometimes they can be trying to pull the wool over our eyes, or trying to evade another writing task, but most of the time, I find, their work fills me with awe.

## Revisiting Essential Unit Question

### What Is the Power of Language?

Language is a way to communicate similarity and differences. This is significant because identifying and communicating contrasts, or our areas of disagreement, is the first step in resolving them or finding acceptable compromise. Identifying similarities in strengths or interests is a step in the direction of unifying and building partnerships.

> Identifying similarities in strengths or interests is a step in the direction of unifying and building partnerships.

## References

Lamb, C., & Lamb, M. (1807). *Tales from Shakespeare*. Juvenile Library of William Godwin.

National Governors Association Center for Best Practices & Council of Chief State School Officers. (2010). *Common core state standards for English language arts and literacy in history/social studies, science, and technical subjects*.

Shakespeare, W. (1596). *A midsummer night's dream*.

Shakespeare, W. (1597). *Romeo and Juliet*.

Shakespeare, W. (1601). *Hamlet*.

# 9
# Shakespeare Festival

One of the greatest moments of my teaching career came after a performance of *A Midsummer Night's Dream*. The students, fresh from their performance, were gathered on the carpet of our classroom that still carried whispers of the enchanted forest – twinkling lights, heaps of green gauzes material that had been curtains, and kraft paper trees that had valiantly stood tall for three performances. I wanted them there to hold the magic of studying Shakespeare together for a few more moments. I also had a gift for them. To each member of the cast and crew I handed an inexpensive copy of the complete *A Midsummer Night's Dream*. The students were pleased with the gift, though I was surprised at quite how pleased they were! The shrieks that accompanied the discovery of what the wrapping paper contained shocked me, and the enthusiasm only grew as students frantically flipped through the book trying to find their parts. Students began reading aloud. It was a cacophony of labored pronunciations and gleeful exclamations: "Here's Bottom! Look at Titania's long speech! That was my line! There are even more fairies than we thought!"

There aren't many times when a teacher gets to see the results of their planning and instructional efforts, which is why seeing the kids glowing was so special. In that post-final production moment, I got to see the seed I planted blossom into enthusiasm that will stay with them throughout their lives. How do I know this? Because I still remain in contact with many many many students and reminiscing about the fun we had with the Bard remains a popular topic of conversation. Because Shakespeare is all around us within our English-speaking culture, I also know that the schema built in their minds relative to Shakespeare gets activated and added to even still.

> Because Shakespeare is all around us within our English – speaking culture, I also know that the schema built in their minds relative to Shakespeare gets activated and added to even still.

The student-designed Shakespeare Festival is important to learning goal work presented throughout this resource because it gives the work the kids are doing real meaning. They know that arduous writing assignments about perspective or close readings around character or word choice are designed to support their work as actors and performers. Their study of setting helps them create their vision of Verona, or Elsinore, or an enchanted forest. The Shakespeare Festival is important because having an actual event to manage and design is motivating and engaging.

## Shakespeare Festival and Museum

Students should know from the start that their study of Shakespeare will culminate with a festival that they will design. The festival may have components that you require, for instance, the festival that I have supported has had two main parts: A performance of the stories and a museum of student work. However, decisions beyond those basic academic requirements are made by students. For example, the performance of Shakespeare can take a variety of different forms including the screening of films, the staging of an abbreviated production of the text studied, or a hybrid of live performances, films, and other creative interpretations of Shakespeare's work. I leave this choice to the students. The museum is a display that features student research projects and artifacts of learning produced in other activities throughout their exploration of Shakespeare.

While I share with current students projects done by former students, and I offer a range of project ideas, the choice of project and product are student driven. In addition, all of the additional work that must be done to hold such a festival is completed by teams of students. The large amount of student control is by design because with greater agency and responsibility comes greater engagement.

## Part 1: Performance of the Stories

The learning activities in the previous chapters are demanding, but the culminating task of hosting a festival to showcase their performances and class work has been creatively and socially motivating enough for students that, in my experience, it motivates them through the more challenging work. A key ingredient to the success of this motivational factor is in connecting lessons, discussions, and writing assignments to their performances. If students understand the why behind different learning activities, and see how doing the activity will improve their performance, then the motivation to invest in the work and confidence in their performance will increase. For example, studying Polonius through character analysis and close reading reveals that he is more complex than just a father. Rather it could be argued, he is an opportunist who is willing to betray his daughter's confidence in order to gain a better position at court. In terms more familiar to students, he used his daughter to get more power by doing a favor for Claudius. He proves this when he reveals to Gertrude and Claudius the love letters that were written to Ophelia from Hamlet. Further, as most students sense is true with many adults, not only does he give advice that he himself does not follow, but his advice seems to be given so he can hear himself talk rather than provide true, loving guidance. The lessons reveal the characters' motivations, flaws, and personalities so that students can bring them to life in their performances. A flat understanding of character yields flat performances. Good actors know who their characters are.

They study them so that the character can be accurately portrayed for the audience. Reiterate this point to students, especially during the work students find more challenging in order to sustain motivation. One strategy is to stop the class in the midst of a laborious assignment to ask them how they think this work will improve their performance and the overall quality of the play.

Student performances depend entirely on the interests and comfort level of your students. I have had years in which shy students who were adamantly opposed to a live audience grow confident enough over the course of studying and rehearsing the text to insist that we invite their entire class, families, and school administrators to attend a live performance after all. I have also had a magnificent Tybalt avoid performance day due to stage fright. It is impossible to tell once you start where your class might eventually end up. Accepting this lack of predictability is part of the journey.

In general, I give students two to three options. Option 1 is a traditional theater performance in which one play is performed and produced by all students for a live audience. Option 2 is a film festival in which the entire class stars in and produces one film of an entire play or several short films of selected scenes. Films are shown to a live audience. Option 3 is a theater festival hybrid. In this option some students perform selected scenes in front of a live audience, and some perform in films. I explain to students that the most advanced option with the most professional results is Option 1, but the decision is theirs. After each option is presented, I allow students time to discuss and apply a creative-thinking strategy like SCAMPER (discussed in Chapter 3) or brainstorming to make changes or additions to the options presented. For example, one group of fifth graders liked the idea of a live performance, with the exception of one student who wanted to do a live performance, but did not want to speak during the performance. His brainstorm group suggested that he star as his idol at the time, DJ Khalid, at the Capulets' party.

**FIGURE 9.1** Students put finishing touches on costumes while classmates finish their projects behind the scenes.

Note: In this chapter, an engraving of Shakespeare's face by Charles Droeshout (1623) has been used to protect children's identities in photographs.

## Supporting Students in Adapting the Play

Working with students to create an adaptation of *A Midsummer Night's Dream*, *Romeo and Juliet*, or *Hamlet* is a fantastically rewarding experience for students, but it can also seem like an endeavor that is spectacular on paper, but overwhelming and thus unrealistic to organize for class. My advice is this: Start small and start simple. An adaptation can be created through a variety of strategies, and not all strategies have to be used in the same production!

### Adding Asides
An aside is when an actor speaks directly to the audience, but the other actors do not hear. This can be an excellent way for students to adapt the play by including some of the in role writing they may have done while studying character or point of view in Chapters 3 and 6 of this resource.

### Including Native Language and Culture
Students can specify the cultural identity of their character, and make some or all of the characters bilingual, and change their lines accordingly. Refer to Chapter 5 for supporting activities.

### Resetting
Students may decide to reset their adaptation in a different setting entirely. This might be a modern-day school or a planet in a far-off galaxy. Students would need to consider what else would change if the setting were changed. Refer to Chapter 3 for supporting activities.

### Music and Special Effects
Students may choose to add music or special effects such as sounds and lighting. Encouraging them to do so can support other adaptations. For instance, music selections can alert the audience to a different cultural context or time.

### Revising the End or Adding Additional Scenes
Students may not agree with the choices made by characters, so allowing them to create a different ending, or adding scenes which further explore the resolution of the story can be an exciting way for them to adapt the original to their own vision.

## Festival Meeting

The many aspects of staging a production from set and prop design to sound effects and marketing can be managed by students if they are organized well, have clear missions to begin with, and are given sufficient time to accomplish their missions.

Holding brief, but regular, meetings provides the structure needed for student teams to work on their festival responsibilities and share their thinking with classmates so that decisions can be made with consensus after discussion, and problems can be solved with support from all.

In my experience, backwards planning to space out festival meetings has been a successful strategy to ensure that they happen. It is just too easy to skip this meeting part but please, don't! These meetings are some of the magic that makes the resulting festival more meaningful for the students because it allows them to own their learning.

## Performance and Festival Meeting Overview

| Festival Planning Stage | Associated Goals and Tasks |
|---|---|
| Beginning<br>Rate: Twice per week – 10–15 minutes of discussion. As the class progresses, meetings can focus more on the work of their specific team and less around group discussion and decision making. | • Explain that the festival is a celebration at the conclusion of the class' exploration of Shakespeare that includes two parts: A performance and a museum.<br>• The museum will feature displays of artifacts from their exploration as well as individual or group projects.<br>• The performance will be either one live action play, a film, or a collection of scenes filmed or performed live. Inform the students that you are willing to consider other ideas they may have.<br>• Inform students of project options. Inform the students that you are willing to consider other ideas they may have.<br>• Collect student feedback regarding their project and performance preferences.<br>• Inform students of, or brainstorm with students to determine, festival team options. Form teams. |

| Festival Planning Stage | Associated Goals and Tasks |
|---|---|
| Middle<br>Rate: Two sessions per week, for a total of about 60 minutes.<br>As students progress with their exploration of Shakespeare and are working towards learning goals, the class will identify, or can be led to identify, different ways in which they might make adaptations to the script.<br>Meeting time will need to be used to discuss these possibilities and make decisions. After major decisions have been made, and teams have been created, roughly 15 minutes of this weekly meeting time is allotted to team updates. During team updates, each team shares the progress they have made towards their particular goals, seeks input from the class, and explains what they intend to accomplish during the week's work time. This routine helps keep students on task during the less structured time in which teams work on their slice of the production because they know they will be held accountable by their peers. This is also an excellent opportunity to informally access speaking and listening goals!<br>Teams spend the remaining 45 minutes working on their specific production tasks related to set design, costumes, props etc.<br>End<br>Rate: One full class session per week to complete team specific production tasks related to set design, costumes, props etc. as needed. | • Determine the setting of the performance, and if other elements of the text will be adapted.<br>• Determine which team will be responsible for which elements of the adaptation, and what tasks will need to happen in order for the updates to occur. For instance, a class in which 80% of students speak Spanish as their home language may want to set their story in Mexico City and have some characters speak certain lines in Spanish. Adjustments to the scripts would need to be made and setting plans would need to be specified prior to starting rehearsals. The class as a whole should make the decisions, but then implementing would be up to the individual teams during time allotted by the teacher to such work.<br>• Teams begin a routine of sharing out their progress, setting new team goals, and using the work time to accomplish those goals during weekly festival planning meeting.<br>• Students not working on a specific team task can also use this time to complete their individual projects.<br>• As the festival and performance approach, students should devote all of the available meeting time to complete their team tasks and individual projects. |

## Festival Planning and Production Teams

I advise organizing students into four different teams or committees: Audio Visual, Backstage and Settings, Costumes, and Marketing. The responsibilities of each team are listed.

### Audio Visual (AV)
- In a classroom equipped with a projector and screen, students can use images found online, and projected behind students to help create the setting. Students on the AV team are in charge of creating the slides to organize the images if this is an option students want to use. During meetings students on the AV team can share found images, or gather suggestions from their classmates, or seek approval of collected images that the team would like to use in the production.
- Similarly, this team can be in charge of any sound effects that can be used to enhance the story. Examples from past productions include playing a rooster's crow when the four friends awake in *A Midsummer Night's Dream*. The sound of metal hitting metal was used to great effect during the sword fights in *Romeo and Juliet*. As with the setting images, the AV team is responsible for sharing sound effect ideas with the class and gathering ideas from their peers to be shared during play meetings for approval. After having selected sound effects approved by their peers the AV team is also responsible for organizing the selected sound effect files into a format that is organized and easily played during the performance or film recording. I suggest a document with links or if background images are to be projected then the sounds can simply be attached to those slides for playback at the appropriate time.
- The AV team might also manage music or songs to be played during the performance in the same way that they would manage sound effects and background images.
- Finally, in the case of film work, and if the resources are available, the AV team would be in charge of any green screen work: Setting up and taking down the screen, preparing background images for use with the green screen, and creating the final green screen footage. This is a perfect place to collaborate with tech staff if your school community has such a resource.

## Backstage and Settings
- Students on the Backstage and Settings team are in charge of organizing the setting designs. While all students will need to contribute to creating the settings and props, the Backstage and Settings keep track of which items need to be created and who is creating them as well as progress to completion.
- The Backstage and Settings team is also in charge of setting up materials for rehearsals and performances, and making sure the stage is reset and ready.

## Costumes
- Students on the Costume team are in charge of organizing and making costumes. As with the setting, all students will be responsible for collecting items from home, or wearing a certain thing such as a dress or a solid color top and bottom, but the team is in charge of keeping track of which items need to be created, who is creating them, and who is bringing what from home.
- The Costume team is also in charge of reporting back to the class the progress being made towards costume completion.

## Marketing
- The Marketing team is responsible for creating posters for display in the school advertising the festival, for creating invitations to send to classrooms and other school leaders, as well as to the families of students performing.
- The Marketing team also sets up the classroom theater chairs, welcomes guests, and announces the start of the performance.

## Performance Materials

One of the most motivating factors of working with Shakespeare, or any theater performance, is the creative opportunities presented by performing a show. Shows require materials for the creation of setting and costumes. The materials you select will of course depend on the decisions made by students. Did they choose to update or adapt the text to reset it? If so, consider those decisions when spending on materials. I've found for most shows, the wildest dreams students have for settings can be achieved through a few rolls of craft paper, basic tempera paints, construction paper, plus boxes and other materials scavenged from home. Glitter is always a hit, but that one clearly depends on your comfort level.

As far as spending on special items, I have found two or three pairs of the heaviest weight 3M hooks I can afford, a package of clothes pins, and some lightweight, but sturdy string make very versatile setting support in any classroom. Use the hooks to hang a length of string. This length represents the front part of your stage. The stage itself can be marked by painter's tape about two to three feet in front of this first clothes line. Hang a second line, leaving about three feet between the first and second line, and a third leaving another three feet between lines. Make sure there is also about three feet behind the last line. This should provide a stage foot print that is about 10 to 12 feet deep. The width of your stage will depend on the dimensions of the scenery your students create and hang on the clotheslines. The lines will allow scenery panels to move forward and back as needed. Layers allow panels to be hidden until needed.

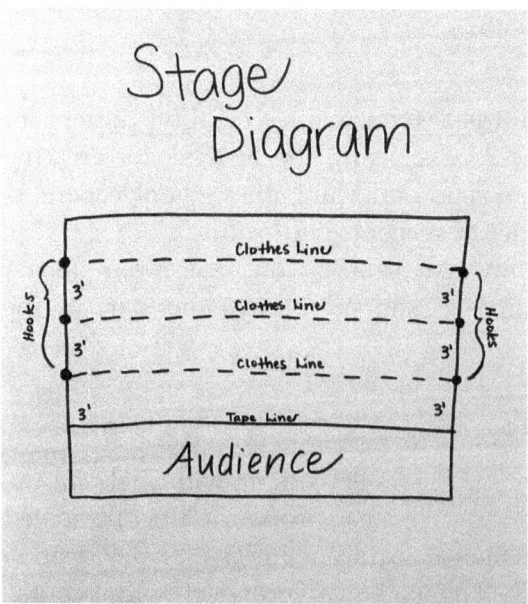

**FIGURE 9.2** This diagram illustrates how to affix temporary hooks and clotheslines from which elements of the setting can be hung. Multiple lines allow elements to be swung in and out of place.

In *Hamlet*, Elsinore's turrets can be fashioned from recycled boxes, and favorite dresses get a chance to shine as the fashion of courtiers. Flashlights taped around the waist of the ghost of King Hamlet create an eerie glow when worn underneath a white cape fashioned from some cheap fabric or an old sheet. In *A Midsummer Night's Dream* the forests can be made more "fairy like" with the addition of holiday lights. Fairy skirts worn over leggings can be whipped together with some tulle fabric and ribbon, but the *piece de resistance* is the rubber donkey mask worn by Bottom when Puck turns him into an ass. Performances of *Romeo and Juliet* have been enhanced by recycling my own bridal veil and tiara, but white tulle and a sparkly hair clips do just as fine. Swords are a must, and are usually made out of cardboard and aluminum foil, although many productions have been outfitted with the toys of students' younger siblings. Making administrators aware of the play and associated props ahead of time, and requiring materials to be brought to the classroom and stored there until they are returned home, has thus far helped me avoid troubles with props such as swords, and daggers.

A theater project just begs for extra materials, so when the resources were available I have indulged productions with some special ingredients. Again though, wait to see what vision students have before investing in any of the items described. It's much more fun to see where the students want to take the production and support that rather than forcing their hand by showing off special materials that might drive their thinking rather than their own ideas. I notice that such a move impacts momentum and the team energy because when we, the boss, inserts himself or herself the kids lose autonomy, and it is with autonomy that engagement loves to dance.

## Part 2: The Museum

As the class moves closer to the performance date, rehearsals should begin to require more class time. I have found the best performances arise out of practices that start by slowly progressing through the text with consecutive rehearsals of scenes, and some rehearsals focused on one scene alone. This proposes a management challenge: How can students who are not rehearsing use their class time meaningfully? The solution I've found most engaging for student, and thus the most behaviorally and academically successful, involved independent or team research projects based on student interest.

In the iteration that was most successful and least time consuming to organize, there were only two requirements required to get a project topic approved. One was that students chose a topic that was at least tangentially related to Shakespeare. This was so that we could continue to build the wide schema of our main topic. And, two, they had to complete a project proposal in which they explained what they were going to be researching, what resources they planned to use, and what product they would produce in order to demonstrate their learning.

At the start of our Shakespeare study students have limited research project time to explore project options, free read, and construct learning webs on the topic, generate questions, and complete their project proposal. As the class moved closer to the performance date when rehearsal requirements increased in time, students who were not in a scene being rehearsed during class were occupied with working on their self-selected projects, so by the time students are required to work entirely independently they are able to do so. An additional accountability tip during this time is to develop an exit ticket for students working on their projects independently while others are rehersing. The one I used was two prompts long: Today I accomplished… and, Next time I will… This keeps agency firmly in the hands of students while also allowing the teacher to monitor productivity.

I've found the most meaningful way to share projstudent projects has been to set up a Shakespeare Research Project Museum for schoolmates, visitors, and families of students to peruse either before or immediately after the class performance. Often, student questions generated during the close readings of the Mary and Charles Lamb stories as described in Chapter 2, can yield interesting topics for research. Below are several descriptions of projects children have selected in the past. Use these ideas as they are or as inspiration.

## What Else Was Going On in the World?

I once had a class of 12 students with whom I got to explore Shakespeare. Within that group of 12, there were 9 different home languages spoken and 11 different cultural heritages represented by 12 children. This class was fueled by connections made between our shared experiences in class and their own experiences. Such connections were often made with the help of a world map which allowed us to make the abstract more concrete. This was a worldly class, and it was with this class that a conversation similar to this was had.

*Student:* Shakespeare. Pretty important, and I'm like glad to know him, but like were the lights off in the rest of the world?

*Teacher:* I'm so glad you asked. This is a really smart question. In this room alone we know about Mexico, Guatemala, Turkey, Poland, Romania, Peru, Palestine, Philippines, the United States, and India. While Shakespeare was writing and his works were being performed, there were things going on all over the world as well. That sounds like an amazing idea to explore. Putting so much focus on this one person can make it seem as if nothing else important or worthwhile was happening, but we can prove that was not the case.

*Student:* Yeah, it's not like the rest of the world was just frozen in time.

*Teacher:* Or busy with a zombie apocalypse. Anyway… Can anyone name something, or someone, or some event that took place during Shakespeare's life?

*Students: (All look around, trying to find someone who can answer…)*

*Teacher:* Can anyone tell me when Shakespeare was born? Or died? Check back in notes, consult Google. Do what you need to to get the info we need to get started!

*Student:* He was born in, well, baptized, so we think born in 1564.

*Student 2:* Aaaaaaaand we think he died in… 1616.

*Teacher: (Makes a simple timeline starting with 1564 and ending with 1616 on the board or on chart paper).* Okay. Now we have a timeframe. Let's do some internet research to answer this question: What also was going on in the world between 1564 and 1616?

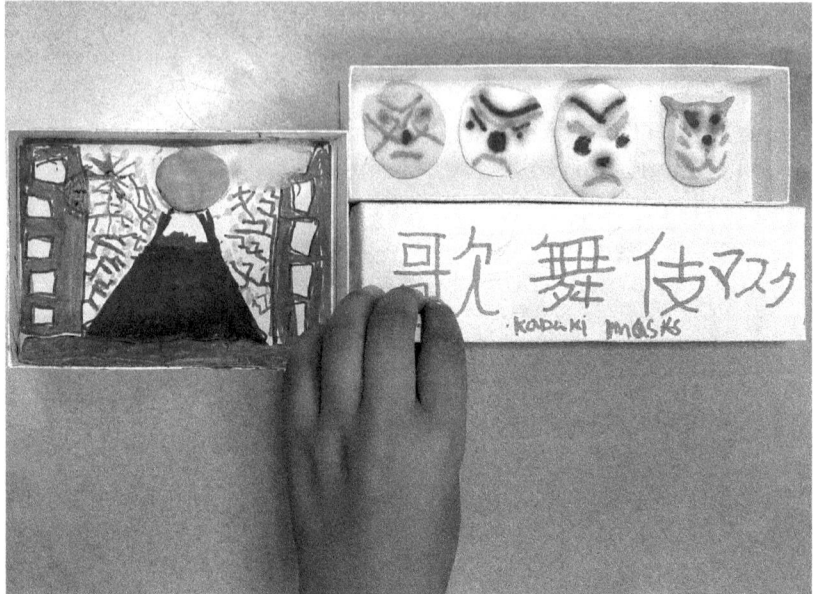

**FIGURE 9.3** A student arranges the visual elements of his research project on Japanese kabuki theater masks ahead of visitors arriving at the Shakespeare Festival Museum.

As a result of this investigation students uncover topics which are added to a list from which all students may select. Such topics include Kabuki theater in Japan, the lost colony at Roanoke in the United States, Galileo's development of the telescope, Sir Francis Drake's raids on Panama and Chile during his expedition to circumnavigate the world, Martin Ignacio De Loyola becoming the first to circumnavigate the world twice, and the fall of the Inca. This particular project is an empowering opportunity for students to build on their understanding of world history, while also developing agency and their own personal cultural identity.

### Shakespeare versus Cervantes

One other interesting answer to the question "what was going on in the world besides Shakespeare?" for students to explore is Cervantes. Miguel de Cervantes Saavedra was born in Spain a bit earlier than Shakespeare, in 1547, and died the same year, 1616. During that time he became the author of *Don Quixote*, the first modern novel and is widely accepted as the greatest writer in the

Spanish language. Students interested in Cervantes can explore a variety of different roads.

- Read an appropriate edition and version of *Don Quixote de La Mancha* and compare it to the Shakespearean story being performed.
- Research the life of Cervantes and Shakespeare and be inspired to write a scene of a historical fiction account of Cervantes and Shakespeare meeting in a park or library on the date of your choice, or a rap battle in which both writers speak of their characters and accomplishments.

## Word Dictionary

After engaging in the English word tree and the dictionary project some students may want to engage more deeply with that word work. These students might be interested in developing a dictionary of made up words that include Greek and Latin roots and are connected by a common theme. For instance, a student whom I got to study Shakespeare with during the summer of 2022 completed a dictionary of types of fairies working for Titania. Other students have completed dictionaries of magical worlds, monsters, and other topics related to setting that were then used as the basis for a variety of student written stories. By doing such a project, students develop a deeper understanding of Greek and Latin roots which are key to developing a robust college ready vocabulary.

## Literature Study

There are several historical fiction books written for 9–13-year-olds that also involve Shakespeare. These books can be used to run literature circles. Students who engage in this work for their personal research might participate in a panel discussion during the festival, create animated summaries or dramatic re-enactments of scenes, or create a trailer for the book read and discussed. These books have also served as starting points for further research. For instance, one of the texts grapples with this question: Did Shakespeare actually write all of these stories? Students engaged by that question completed a project explaining their perspective and sharing evidence that they found to support their thinking.

*Shakespeare's Secret* by Elisa Broach
*The Shakespeare Mysteries Series* by Deron R. Hicks and Mark Edward Geyer
*Wicked Will: A Mystery of Young William Shakespeare* by Bailey MacDonald
*The Shakespeare Stealer Series* by Gary L. Blackwood
*King of Shadows* by Susan Cooper

### Student Developed Project

In order to support student agency, I also like to provide students with the opportunity to develop their own projects. However, experience has taught me that having some basic expectations and requirements in place leads students to create at a higher quality level than if I were to simply let them run wild. Below is a list of questions and requirements that students must address through their project proposal. If students are working on specific learning goals, and you would like evidence of those goals being successfully reached within their project, then expectations related to those goals may be added to the following list.

1. Connection: Your research project must explain how this project relates to our study of Shakespeare.
2. Questions: Your research project must answer three separate research questions, one of which must be this question: What is the power of language? The other two questions must be student developed.
3. Research: You will need to do research. Find at least two or three texts to answer each of your research questions. Sources will need to be approved.
4. Visual: Your project will need to include a visual element, for example: a speech delivered as if you were the person, an animation, graphs and charts, models, or any other visual that will help your audience understand and be engaged by your presentation.
5. Presentation: You will need to speak on your findings for one to three minutes.

## Final Assessment

If a final assessment is a desired element of your exploration of Shakespeare, then there are a variety of possibilities available. One option is to develop a traditional assessment that is based on learning goals targeted during your exploration of Shakespeare, and consists of text dependent questions that students answer by stating a claim and providing supporting text evidence. Another option is to have students create an essay response to the unit's essential question: What is the power of language?

Students can either express a personal philosophical answer that represents the power they see in language, or they might explain what Shakespeare has taught them about the power of language trough his dramatic works. Other possibilities include a portfolio review of work done in conjunction with learning goals, peer reviews, and their participation in the production.

## A Few Words in Closing to My Kind Reader, the Educator

I am not, by any means, an expert on Shakespeare. The path to exploring the Bard with my students has a sordid start that involves not only the Shakespeare Insult Generator but also my deepest teacher secret. I hate *Charlotte's Web*. I lived with this shame for three years. By the fourth year, the thought of having to keep Wilbur's voice distinct from Charlotte's as I modeled fluency for the students made me want to run away screaming. Plus, I resent the guilty feelings the book gives me about eating bacon. Feeling hostile about teaching *Charlotte* trickled into how I was feeling about other areas of instruction too. Good Lord. Long division and *Charlotte's Web*? During the same month? As my four-year-old nephew said when offered a barely roasted whole quail by my father on Christmas Eve, "No, please."

Teaching elementary students can be mind-numbing if we do not introduce novelty for our students and the challenge of integrating new material for ourselves. I started down this path partly because I needed a change. I needed to feel excited about something I was doing in the classroom. My greatest hope is that this resource sparked something that energized you. Perhaps it is teaching the Bard, or creating a culminating festival, or perhaps it is seeing how you can turn student interests into administration pleasing lessons that make you want to be in the classroom exploring with your students while also teaching literacy goal aligned lessons.

> *If we shadows have offended,*
> *Think but this, and all is mended,*
> *That you have but slumbered here*
> *While these visions did appear.*
>
> *– Puck*
> *William Shakespeare*
> *A Midsummer Night's Dream*

## References

Lamb, C., & Lamb, M. (1807). **Tales from Shakespeare**. Juvenile Library of William Godwin.

Shakespeare, W. (1596). ***A midsummer night's dream***.

Shakespeare, W. (1597). ***Romeo and Juliet***.

Shakespeare, W. (1601). ***Hamlet***.

# About the Author

**Jennifer Szwaya** has served several school districts in the suburbs of Chicago as a classroom teacher, a gifted specialist, and instructional coach. Teaching Shakespeare to her students has been a passion project for the duration of her career. When she is not busy in elementary schools, Jennifer can be found scavenging yard sales and discount shops to find those extra touches for the Shakespeare Festival such as rubber chickens, yards of green tulle fabric, and old wedding dresses. Jennifer lives outside of Chicago with her husband and two dogs Leonidas and Maximus. More information about her work can be found online at www.jenniferszwaya.com.

For Product Safety Concerns and Information please contact our EU
representative GPSR@taylorandfrancis.com
Taylor & Francis Verlag GmbH, Kaufingerstraße 24, 80331 München, Germany

www.ingramcontent.com/pod-product-compliance
Lightning Source LLC
Chambersburg PA
CBHW052016290426
44112CB00014B/2266